# PORPHYRIOS
## ASSOCIATES

NA MONOGRAPHS

# PORPHYRIOS
## ASSOCIATES

### RECENT WORK

ANDREAS PAPADAKIS PUBLISHER

FRONT COVER AND FRONTIS: THE DAKIS JOANNOU COLLECTION GALLERIES
BACK COVER AND PAGE FIVE: THREE BRINDLEYPLACE OFFICE BUILDING

*This monograph would not have been possible without the contribution over the past five years of all who have worked in our Practice. We are most grateful to Professor Paolo Portoghesi, historian, architect and professor of architecture at the University of Rome and to Dr. Oswyn Murray, Fellow and Tutor at Balliol College, Oxford for writing the introductory essays. Special thanks are due to the publisher Dr. Andreas Papadakis, to Andrea Bettella for the design of the layout, and to Nigel Cox and Nicky Walker for their editorial competence and enthusiasm.*

First Published in Great Britain in 1999 by
ANDREAS PAPADAKIS PUBLISHER
An imprint of NEW ARCHITECTURE GROUP LTD
107 Park Street, London W1Y 3FB

ISBN 1-901092-13-5  PB
ISBN 1-901092-14-3  HB

Printed and bound in Singapore

# C O N T E N T S

# INTRODUCTION

## OSWYN MURRAY

Architects are mostly concerned with two aspects of their buildings. The first is the dynamics of space and technology; the second concerns the functional organisation of their buildings. Few architects ever consider the third element which is always present in architecture: its relationship to time. Indeed they often seek to exclude the element of time from their work. The result is to privilege formalist design over use and life and to produce curiously unreal buildings.

We all live in time, and architects hope that their buildings will survive in time. Time brings both decay and change of use. On old buildings, however, we usually admire decay and ageing because traditional materials age graciously and it is possible to predict what a brick will look like, and how stone, slate or wood will behave over time. Architects also hope that their buildings will live on, but do not concern themselves with making amends with tradition so that they may participate in the metaphysical flow of time, and make a connection with future time.

Both of these techniques are used by Demetri Porphyrios in his buildings. Traditional forms and traditional materials serve to relate his buildings to the flow of time, to mediate between the sense of newness and the life of the existing urban fabric; he goes even further in adapting his architecture to historical context, continuing, for example, the Spetses vernacular at Pitiousa or the mixture of classical and gothic which has marked the buildings of Magdalen College, Oxford from the middle ages to the 1920s. In his use of form he does not seek to provide ideal models, but rather to reflect the character and imperfections of the context in which he finds himself. His architecture at Pitiousa and Magdalen College is neither purist revival nor allusively modern, but placed in history and contextualised. As such it alludes to past continuities, and invites continuation in the future.

But Porphyrios seeks also to relate presentation of space to the continuities of time by incorporating an element of the fortuitous or unplanned into situations which might otherwise seem to demand symmetry and axiality. By incorporating the accidental into the plans of his Magdalen College buildings, by varying the buildings and setting them at angles, Porphyrios seeks to allude to the effects of time and chance and to suggest a reading of the buildings as developing over time.

Porphyrios is a master of the engagement with time; and it is this which provides a theoretical context and a justification for his allusions to history and context. His architecture situates itself in the interplay between history as accident and history as changing function. The very ludic quality of his engagement with time, the sense in which he is playing with it and lures us into it, derives from his fascination with and respect for the importance of time in architecture. Deeply conscious of history and place and always striving to move both heart and mind, Porphyrios' architecture is built on his mastery of the engagement with time.

THREE BRINDLEYPLACE

OFFICE BUILDING,

DETAIL OF THE

CORINTHIAN ORDER

# CLASSICISM IN MANHATTAN

PAOLO PORTOGHESI

O ver the past ten years, Demetri Porphyrios has been recognised internationally as one of the most defiant proponents of classical humanism. His polemical writings and buildings stem directly from his radical opposition to the debilitating practices of contemporary modernist and post-modernist architecture and urbanism.

His radicalism in striving to annul the almost universal hegemony of modernism can be compared with the brave rebellion ushered in by the architects of the avant-garde – from Le Corbusier and Van Doesburg to Mies – who in the early decades of this century precipitated a crisis against the prevailing architectural culture.

Initiating a renaissance of humanist architecture, however, may be a much harder choice than the one made by the modernist avant-garde, primarily because humanism today is *in extremis*. And yet, Porphyrios' analysis of the modernist city and of the life-demeaning implications of the contemporary building industry has highlighted a number of indisputable failures of modernist industrial culture. It is by no means certain, of course, how the debate between an architecture of humanism and that of expediency and technophilia will develop in the future. For the moment, what is difficult to deny is the substance and quality present in Porphyrios' work. His work has come to public attention and praise not only for its radicalism but equally so

TOWN OF

PITIOUSA,

SPETSES,

DETAILS OF

PERGOLA

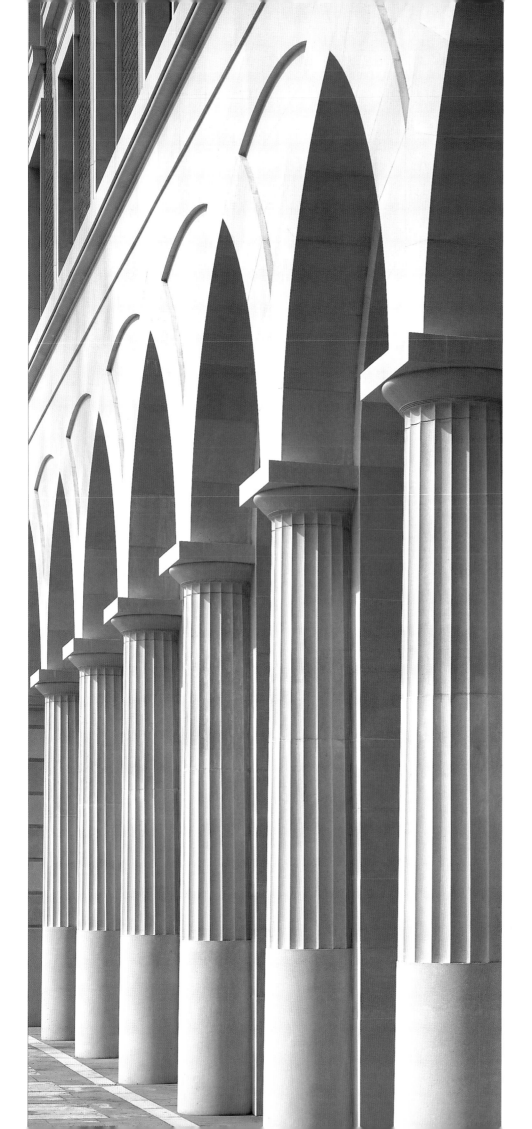

THREE BRINDLEYPLACE
OFFICE BUILDING,
DETAIL OF THE
DORIC COLONNADE

for the fascination it offers in reinterpreting the classical tradition with a freshness and strength that appeals to our contemporary sensibilities.

The post-modernist sixties and seventies accustomed us to contextualism, historicist quotations and ironic witticisms. Robert Venturi, in particular, popularised the use of quotation and irony as rhetorical figures. Classical fragments were used to express our detachment and, thereby, our nostalgia for things that had already passed away and which could be recalled but never experienced in reality.

Porphyrios, in contrast to Venturi, theorises instead on a 'return to the antique,' a new renaissance similar to many others which, from Charlemagne onwards, have formed the history of western art. Porphyrios turns to the antique not in order to revive a bygone form of society or a way of living and thinking as has been the case with revivalist movements. The resurrection of a pure past is historically impossible since the past cannot be considered as given but as something to be attained and constructed by the modernity of its present. Instead, what Porphyrios draws from the antique is the recognition that tradition is always constructed as a form of distancing and differentiation rather than as an immutable continuity with the past.

For Porphyrios, architecture derives its language from the exemplars of human civilisation which, over the centuries, enrich and multiply through an infinite series of creative interpretations.

At the same time, architecture speaks of the tectonics of its construction; in other words, the forms of architecture acquire their authority and consensual codes of recognition not from the technical function which produced them but, rather, from the exemplary and paradigmatic status that social mythology and symbolism confers upon them. "It is not for pleasure but out of necessity that our temples have gables," wrote Cicero. "The need to discharge rainwater has suggested their form. And yet, such is the beauty of their form that if one were to build a temple on Mount Olympus – where I am told it never rains – one would still feel obliged to crown it with a pediment."

Whether in London, Athens or Manhattan, the humanist architecture of Porphyrios represents an origin that has been already destroyed and which requires the mediation

of exile and reconstruction. That is why his architecture has the freshness of a forgotten story that is now being invented anew. In his early houses in London and Athens, his resort town in Spetses, or in his university buildings in Oxford and Cambridge, the philological rigour of the scholar has nothing of pedantry. In each case the formal inventions appear natural without imposition or affectation and the discovery of ancient words imparts a freshness and brilliance to the architecture.

At the same time, the harmonious connection between architecture and urban form is, perhaps, one of the fundamental characteristics of Porphyrios' work. His New York Pavilion in Battery Park City relates unexpectedly to the surrounding skyscrapers without being diminished or lost. The pavilion raises itself above mere technical function offering, as it does, a poetic praise of tectonics.

Today many cultured architects cuddle in glossy magazines, embalming themselves in minimalism and technophilia. In contrast to this medley of 'gregotissmo,' stands the humanist architecture of Porphyrios. In his search for form, Porphyrios does not stop at a diagrammatic minimalism but he probes into the heart of the classical and produces an architecture that has fullness and maturity. His architecture – paradoxically, much like the work of very different architects, such as Gehry and Ando, for example – participates in the search for the new without making the new an idol for veneration.

The work of Porphyrios has a charisma of the absolutely formal, a quality of creativity and invention which finds itself not in academic repetitions but in the classical as a way of life. His work has a spontaneity and a capacity to adapt itself to a place, and of expressing the harmony between man and nature.

*A version of this essay was first published in the Italian newspaper* L'Informazione, *14th March, 1995.*

Town of Pitiousa,

Spetses,

Details of Pergolas

# TOWN OF PITIOUSA

SPETSES, *1993*

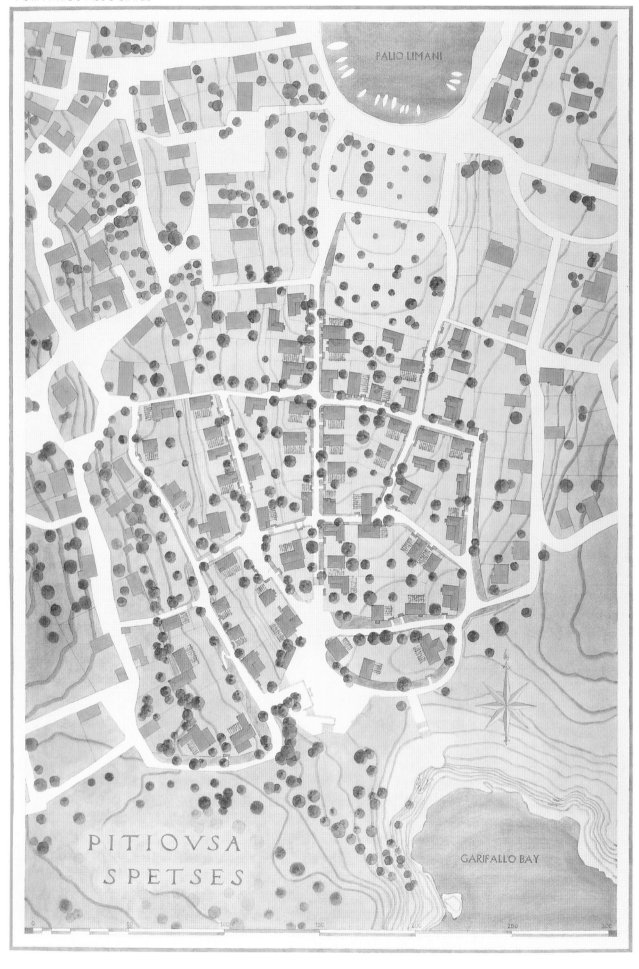

PALIO LIMANI

PITIOVSA
SPETSES

GARIFALLO BAY

LOCATION

PLAN;

CONTEXTUAL

IMAGES

T he island of Spetses, with its magnificent
pine woods, has a most salubrious climate
and in the town still stand the classico-vernacular
mansions of sea captains and mariners from the
nineteenth century. Pitiousa is at the eastern end of
the town, occupying the upper part of the land that
rises gently from the old harbour and falls steeply to
Garifallo bay. The masterplan extends the existing urban fabric by
projecting a network of streets that converge at the highest point on a
square overlooking the rocky escarpment of the sea. The design for the
town of Pitiousa recognises that every context is a self-regulating,
living system; that the basic elements of urbanism are the urban block,
the street and the square; that buildings should never be as large as
the commission; and that they should use well-tried constructional
techniques and materials. Pitiousa also recognises that 'Classicism is
not a style' but a tradition that has evolved from and coexisted with
the vernacular. It is a living tradition open to adaptation and interpretation, and
responsive to region, climate and nature. Pitiousa, writes Paolo Portoghesi, "has
a quality of creativity which finds itself not in academic repetitions but in the
classical as a way of life."

VIEW OF

MAIN

STREET

LEADING TO

SQUARE

# STREETS & SQUARES

W e continue to burn our woods and to consult experts for levelling the land. Yet, it is the landscape that enhances our buildings. In it we recognise both absence of grandeur and true grandeur. As we follow the topography of the land we measure the earth through the effort of our body. We cherish the thousand combinations of solid-and-void and of light-and-shadow, the narrow passage opening onto the flat expanse of a valley, we walk under the deep shade of pine trees, and this infinite pleasure which, as we skirt an orchard, comes to us has in it something of a spiritual quality. The landscape offers to urbanism its prototypes. We have, therefore, given great attention to setting the site levels for each plot, retaining the age-worn olive trees that lend a timeless character to the new town, containing the streets with low stone walls, and masterplanning the layout of the streets and square carefully in a perspectival manner. When we spend money in building public open spaces, we invest wisely. Life thrives only when the open, unbuilt spaces are treated with the same care and expense as the buildings themselves.

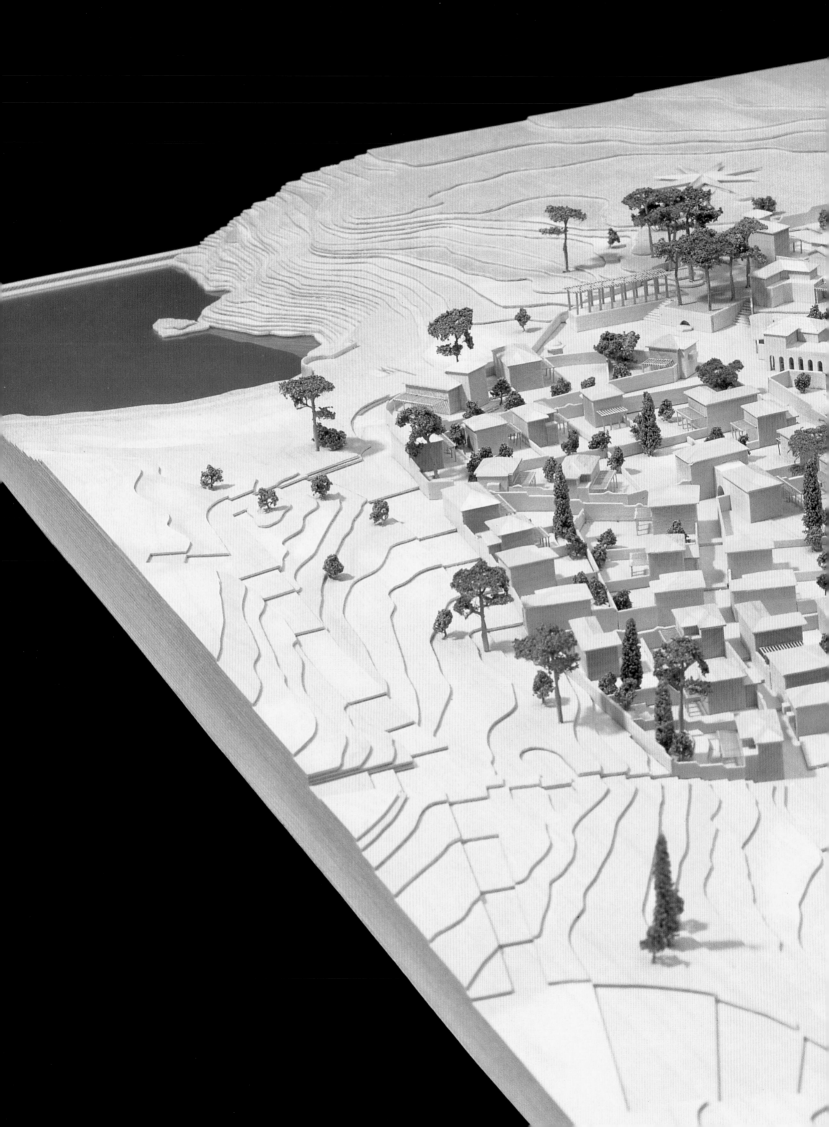

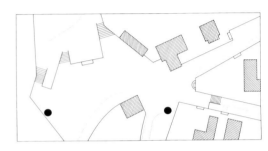

NODE DIAGRAMS AND URBAN VIEWS

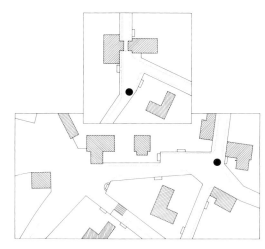

NODE DIAGRAMS AND URBAN VIEWS

VIEW OF MAIN EAST-WEST STREET AND PERSPECTIVE DRAWING

VIEW OF

MAIN

NORTH-SOUTH

STREET

LEADING TO

OLD

HARBOUR

# URBAN BLOCKS

The urban strategy we adopted is that of the existing traditional town of Spetses. Small urban blocks measuring not more than 25x50m or 30x60m are divided into seven to nine plots and are bounded by low stone walls. Most houses are placed at the perimeter of the block, thus defining spatially the street as a public space. The remaining land of the individual plots is then put to good use as private gardens. An intricate system of terracing is formed and particular attention has been given to setting the site levels for each plot, following largely the existing contours and retaining the olive and pine trees. The perimeter boundary walls distinguish between public and private. Entrance is through an honorific gate that opens onto a paved forecourt and shaded pergola from which one enters the house. We must remember that towns and cities are made up of smaller groupings. Such neighbourhoods are both complete in themselves and yet, in the context of the whole town, unfinished. We must always allow for the spatial, formal and functional incidents which connect the parts of a town.

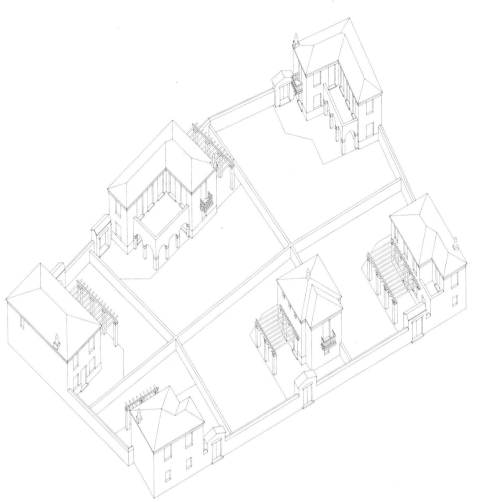

Typical View of a Block and Perspective Drawing

# HOUSES

A small number of house types guarantees the commercial success of the project and the formal cohesion of the new town. The house plans are generally additive or subtractive by using square, rectangular and L-shaped plan forms. The compositional permutations provided by pergolas, balconies, terraces and gates, as well as by the techniques of rotation, reflection and substitution, generate an infinite range of houses. In addition, variation in site conditions, orientation, planting, details and colour have lent sufficient difference to each house to ensure variety while retaining the coherence of the whole. The unity of repetition – as opposed to the unity of the copy – is today an important design consideration. How can we avoid industrial uniformity while eschewing arbitrariness? We must recognise that a repetition is always different from that which it repeats. Such a 'répétition différante' conveys both a sense of the necessary and of freedom. It conveys a sense of the necessary because order is in the rules of design, the materials and the construction used. At the same time it conveys a sense of freedom since the slightest change in the context triggers a chain of modifications which are responsible ultimately for everything that is different. Such 'répétition différante' is at the very centre of nature and it is its laws we must study.

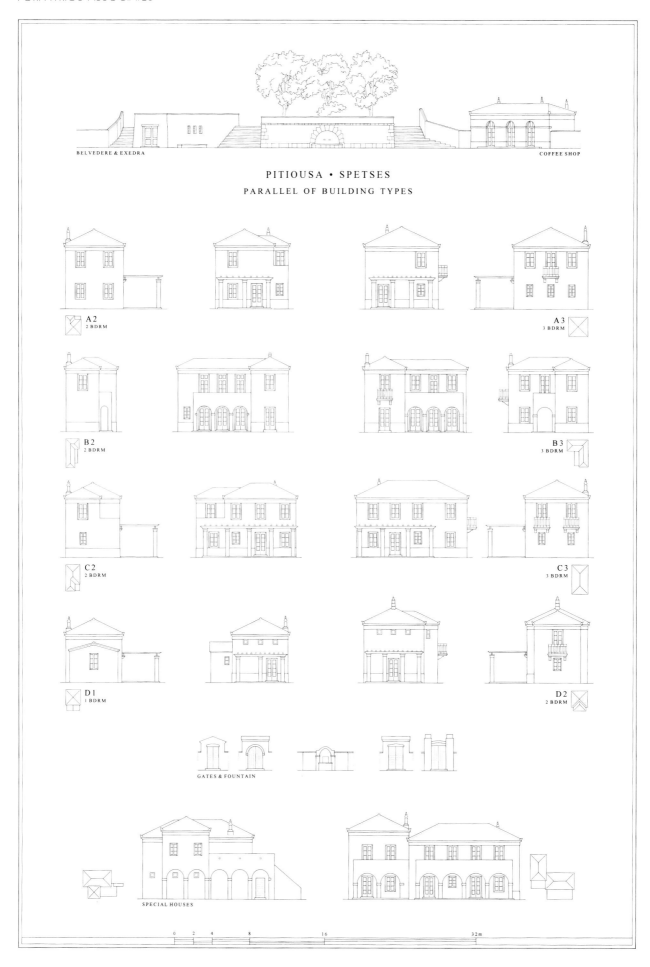

BELVEDERE & EXEDRA

COFFEE SHOP

PITIOUSA · SPETSES

PARALLEL OF BUILDING TYPES

A 2
2 BDRM

A 3
3 BDRM

B 2
2 BDRM

B 3
3 BDRM

C 2
2 BDRM

C 3
3 BDRM

D 1
1 BDRM

D 2
2 BDRM

GATES & FOUNTAIN

SPECIAL HOUSES

0   2   4   8   16   3 2 m

HOUSE TYPE C3: PERSPECTIVE VIEW, FIRST AND GROUND FLOOR PLANS

AXONOMETRIC OF TYPICAL HOUSE

Perspective View of Garden & Pool Pergola

DETAIL OF

PERIMETER

WALL AND

TYPICAL

GATE

# DETAILS & INTERIORS

The town of Spetses has both simple vernacular buildings and larger houses distinguished by their classical treatment. The new buildings of Pitiousa draw knowingly from these traditions and the character of the new town appears inevitable and natural. Similarly, the interiors of the houses are treated in a classico-vernacular manner with single or double-height living areas, exposed timber roofs, panelled ceilings, stone floors and plastered walls. Simple unadorned construction, in keeping with the local character and traditions; based on the expressed aim to enhance existing building traditions rather than destroy them. It is in this sense that we can say that the character of a building is never determined by an individual architect. This is perhaps the case with all architecture. "Pitiousa's surfaces will wear," writes Ian Latham in Architecture Today, "its paintwork will crack and will be repainted, its planting will mature and it will acquire the ad hoc accoutrements that distinguish a piece of real town – it will age with dignity. Because of the way it has been planned, designed and built, the project has an inherent capacity to endure."

PITIOUSA · SPETSES

PARALLEL OF ARCHITECTURAL ELEMENTS

A EXTERIOR CORNICE  B PERGOLA CORBEL  C GABLE CORNICE  D PERGOLA CAPITAL
E DOOR ARCHITRAVE  F DOOR BASE  G PICTURE RAIL  H SKIRTING
I OVER DOOR PANEL  J PRIMARY INTERIOR CORNICE  K SECONDARY INTERIOR CORNICE

DETAILS OF

ROOFS AND

PERGOLAS

WITH THE

SURROUNDING

HILLS IN THE

BACKGROUND

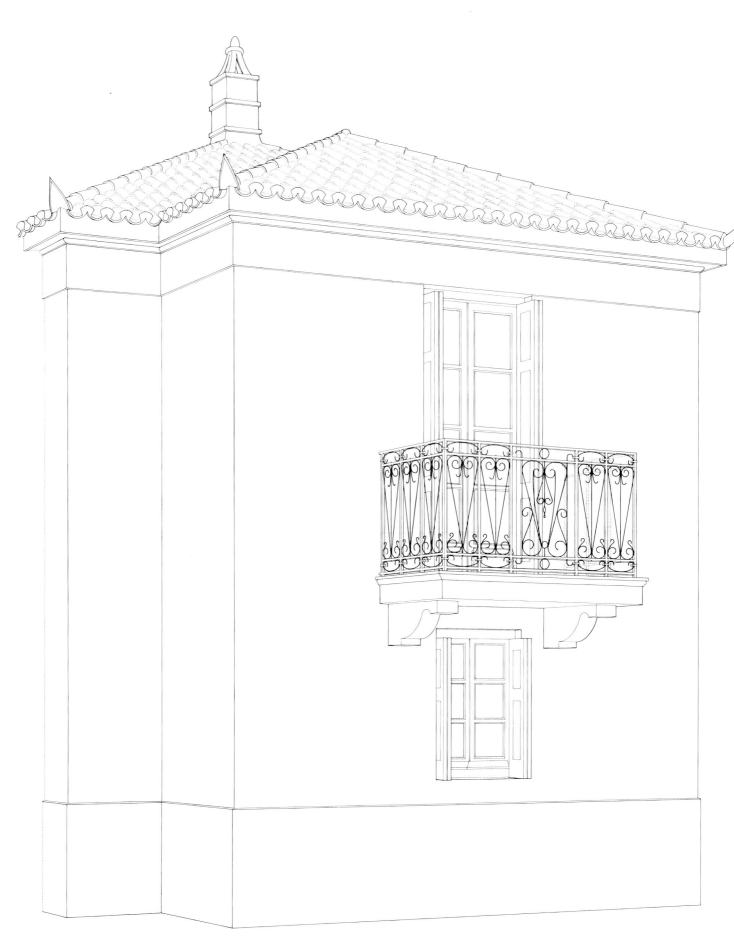

House

Type D2:

Ground and

First floor

Plans

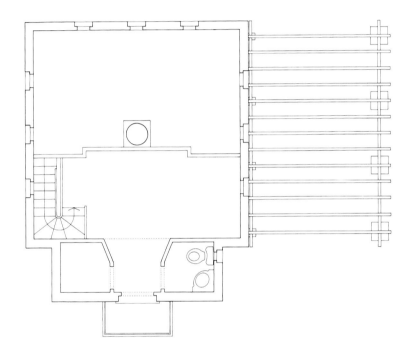

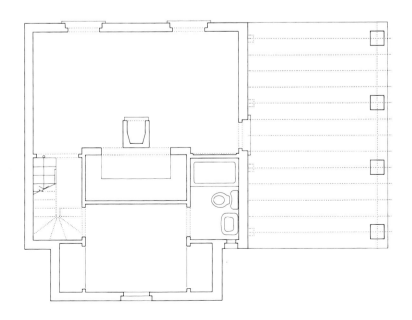

House

Type D2:

Perspective

View and

Interior

Views of

Living

Room and

Gallery

Above

HOUSE

TYPE C3:

INTERIOR

VIEW OF

LIVING

ROOM

# DUNCAN RESIDENCE & GALLERIES
## LINCOLN, NEBRASKA, *1997*

This project is in the great midland plains of North America. It is both a house and a gallery for a client who loves hand-woven baskets and Learjets and who collects modernist abstract sculpture. The siting of the building is both picturesque and surreal. The artificial wooded mound that serves as its backdrop appears as a surreal intrusion in the flatness of the prairie and an unlikely neighbour to the adjacent interstate which it helps mask. A grid of paths is superimposed on the wooded grounds of the estate with its resultant squares planted in different varieties of prairie grass. Amidst this colourful patchwork quilt, where the paths intersect or at the end of their axes the gigantic sculptures are sited. The massing of the building is additive with the principal exhibition and entertaining rooms clustered around a central glazed atrium. A colonnaded courtyard at the north end serves as a carport and service yard. The house has the scale of a gallery and just as the picturesque quality of the estate contrasts with the prairie grid, the Indiana stone of its walls contrasts with the brushed stainless steel windows and doors. This gallery-as-house is pure equivocation occupying as it does the space between public and private. As a gallery it offers refuge from an increasing techno-functional world. At the same time it claims the traditional protective functions of a house associating with the ground and becoming 'natural' to its prairie site.

CROSS

SECTION

THROUGH

ATRIUM AND

GENERAL

SITE

PLAN

DUNCAN RESIDENCE

0 50 100        500        1000Ft

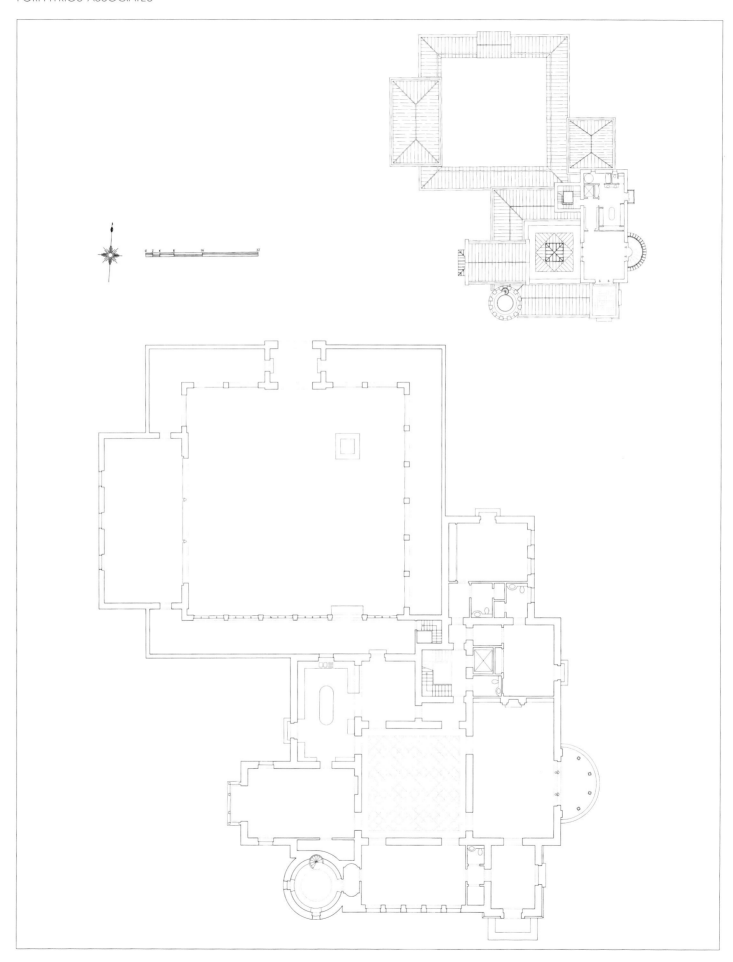

First and

Second

Floor

Plans and

Front

Elevation

# VILLA
# AT PORTO HELI

*1996*

Just opposite the island of Spetses, on the mainland, lies Porto Heli with its surrounding hills covered in pine trees and the green of olives. This stretch of land has
for long been dotted with country villas and seaside retreats. This villa is a place of
otium, or restful leisure, and reference is made here to the tradition of the Graeco-
Roman country villa. Woods, the seasonal winds, views and the sea were all important
to the siting of the villa, which is located on a south-facing hillside overlooking the sea.
The approach is along a meandering road that cuts across the estate travelling parallel to
the coast. Upon entry a peristyle, built above the cisterns, describes a courtyard adjacent
to which a guest house and the villa proper are sited. The peristyle is a most versatile
architectural element that serves as a protective roof, a screen, a filter and a framing
device, lending as it does its regulating presence to all activities within it or beside it.
The villa has rooms of varied shape and height which are arranged in an additive
manner around a central open-air atrium. Exedras, pavilions, a bathing terrace, pergolas and extensive landscaping form its numerous outdoor spaces used at different times
of the day for relaxation and entertaining. The walls externally are finished in yellow
ochre render; the roofs are in clay tiles; oak beams have been used for all exposed roofs
and pergolas, while all retaining walls for the terraces are in local stone. The character of
the villa is classico-vernacular with sparse classical references as in the profiles of cornices
and in the capitals of columns and pilasters.

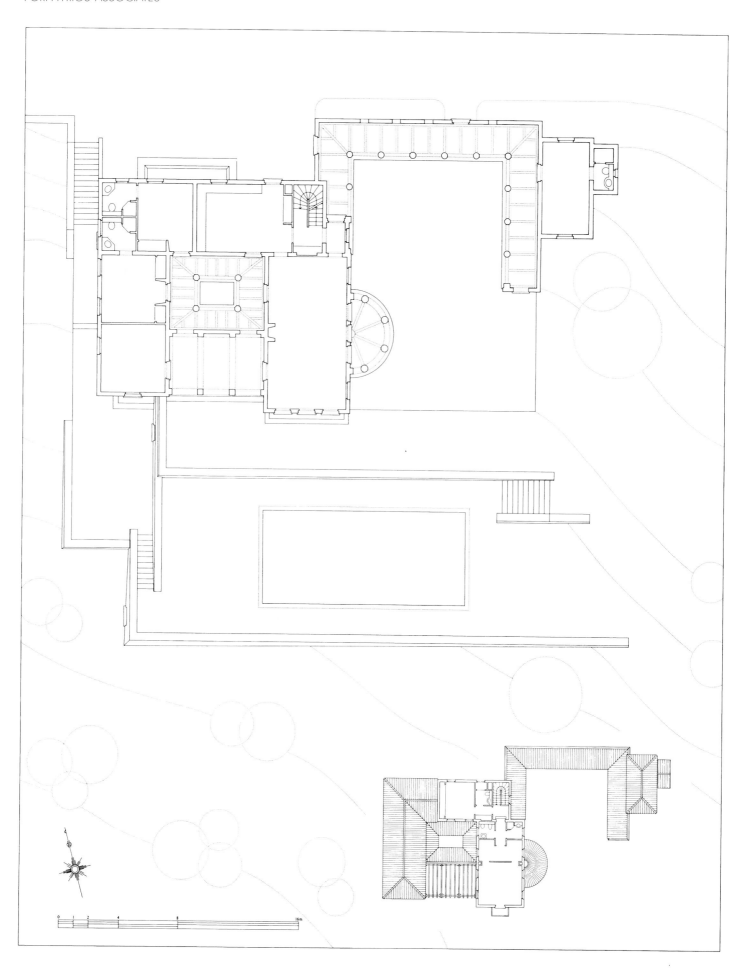

Ground & First

Floor Plans

and

Sectional Elevation

Through

Atrium and

Peristyle

# OLD PALACE SCHOOL

## CROYDON, SURREY, *1997*

The Old Palace School, formerly a residence for the Archbishops of Canterbury, was opened in 1889 by the Sisters of the Church and it is today a member of the Whitgift Foundation. The fifteenth-century Chapel, Great Hall and Library have long been the nucleus of the School's historic buildings, while new accommodation has been built over the

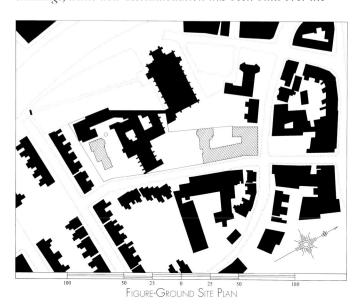

FIGURE-GROUND SITE PLAN

years. The need for permanent buildings, however, to house the preparatory and senior schools has long been recognised. Our aim has been to provide functional, well-built buildings, which impart a sense of reassurance that educational values can and must endure. At the same time, we felt drawn to reconstitute the open spaces of the site into a series of informal courts. By placing the new preparatory and senior schools at opposite ends of the site, two courts are created either side of the Great Hall. The larger court embraces visually the Church of St. John which is drawn into the composition. The buildings of the new preparatory school define the urban block at the intersection of the adjacent streets and form a third, smaller court used exclusively by infants and younger pupils.

# MAGDALEN COLLEGE

GROVE QUADRANGLE, OXFORD, *1994*

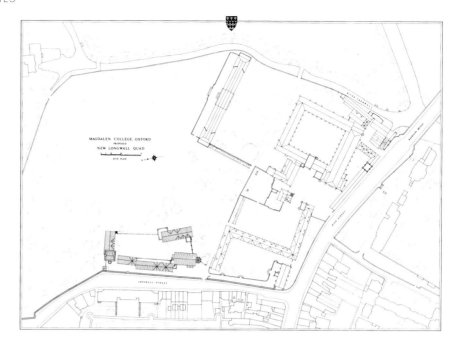

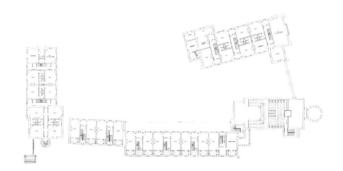

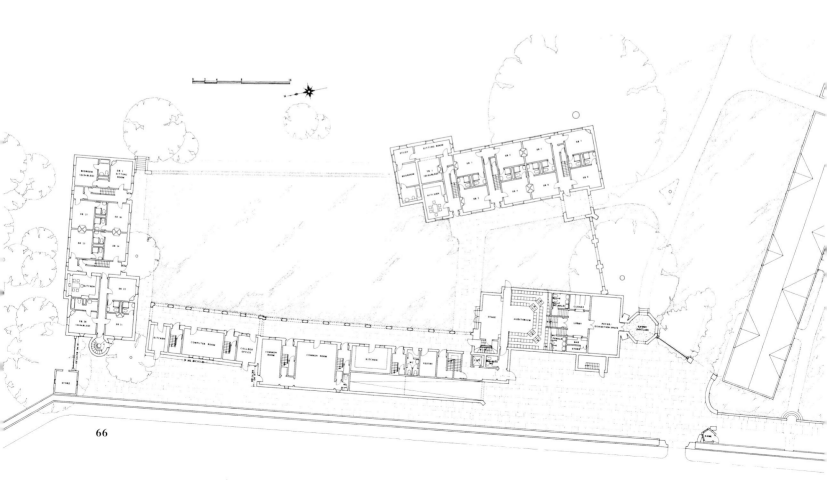

Magdalen College represents, perhaps, the ideal college townscape. Around its fifteenth-century Great Tower and Cloister Quad unfolds an assemblage of buildings and spaces varied in scale and character. "Porphyrios' new Grove Quadrangle," writes Philip Johnson, "is a worthy crown for a great College." It is this urban model of collegiate Oxbridge planning that we adopted in our design. The new buildings are generally composed around a quad which opens to the east towards the deer park. The auditorium is placed close to Longwall Gate thus emphasising its public nature while marking the second most important entrance to the College. In siting the residential buildings we distinguished them into small units to facilitate phasing in construction as well as to give the overall composition the sense of incremental growth over time. Residential accommodation is organised in traditional Oxford sets of two or four rooms per landing. The buildings are constructed in masonry walls with ashlar Ketton stone externally and painted plaster internally. All exposed timber work is in oak. Roofs are generally in stone tiles except the auditorium roof, which is finished in copper. The contrast in scale and character between the classical of the auditorium and the Magdalen vernacular of the residential buildings heightens the dialogue between their public and private nature respectively, thus underlining the urban quality of the scheme and its relation to the existing College.

FIGURE-GROUND PLAN

SHOWING

MAGDALEN COLLEGE

IN CONTEXT

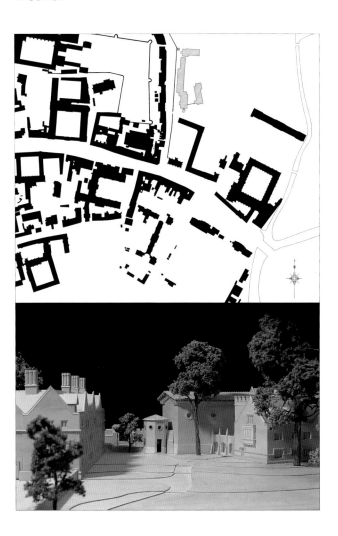

MODEL

SHOWING THE

NEW AUDITORIUM AND

DEER PARK

RANGE

*"Porphyrios' primary concern and his great ingenuity,"* writes *Richard Reid in* Architecture Today, *"is in the design of public space. The concern is less with the Corbusian idea of architecture as 'buildings surrounded by space' than with the definition and modulation of space by means of buildings [. . .] While exploiting the anecdotal nature characteristic of English townscape, Porphyrios gently skews the plan to create a benign fragment that has a degree of conscious incompleteness about it. This planning strategy can cater with the variegated cultural pressures and programmatic constraints of the present [. . .] It is also strong enough visually to provide a coherent image yet charged with a dynamic to which the design of public space makes a vital contribution. Porphyrios recognises this flexibility as an essential ingredient in good city form and succeeds masterfully in providing it here."*

AERIAL PERSPECTIVE VIEW AND MODEL OF THE NEW GROVE QUADRANGLE

ELEVATION AND
VIEW OF THE
LONGWALL RANGE;
INTERIOR VIEW
OF THE
ARCADE

ELEVATION AND VIEWS OF THE DEER PARK RANGE

VIEW OF THE DEER PARK RANGE FROM THE NEW QUADRANGLE

SOUTH ORIEL

WINDOW DETAILS

AND

SOUTH ELEVATION

OF THE

DEER PARK

RANGE

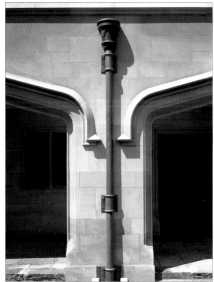

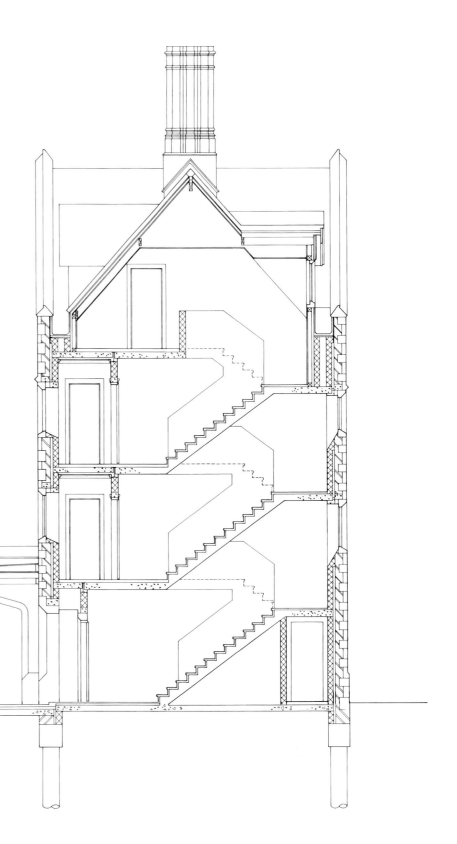

INTERIOR VIEW OF

TYPICAL STAIRCASE

FROM THE

LONGWALL

RANGE

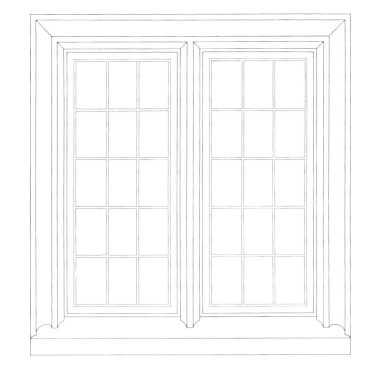

INTERIOR

VIEW OF

TYPICAL

STUDENT

ROOM

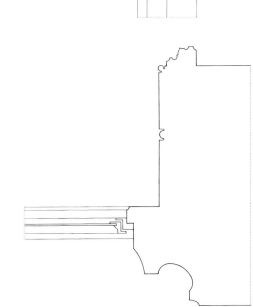

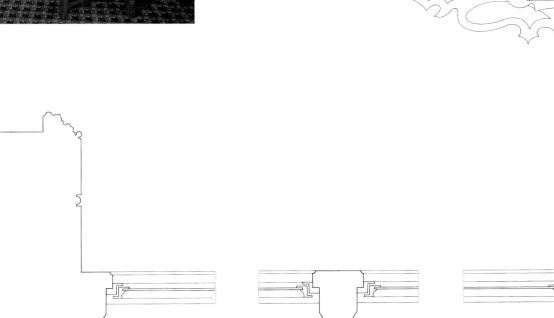

TYPICAL WINDOW DETAILS

VIEW OF THE GREAT TOWER AND THE COLLEGE FROM THE SOUTH ORIEL WINDOW

FELLOWS'

DINING

ROOM

AND

LOCATION

PLAN

# GONVILLE & CAIUS COLLEGE

CAMBRIDGE, *1996*

*W*hen Gonville and Caius College moved its library from Gonville Court to the nearby C.R. Cockerell building, a competition was held to design the interiors of the two rooms of the old library. These were to be used by the College fellows as reading and dining rooms. We envisaged the new reading room as a great hall. Maintaining its existing timbered roof and trusses, we resolved both the structural and organisational requirements in an integral manner where a

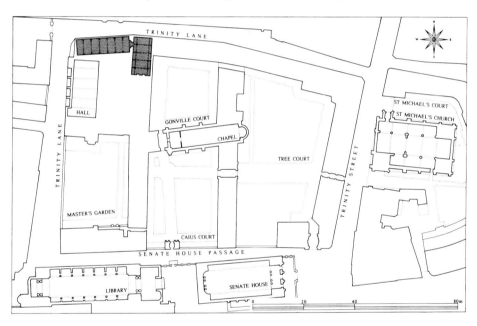

series of side bays for conversation and reading help strengthen the structure of the roof. By contrast, the dining room suggested a trabeated system of construction where the structural relevance of the existing beams is made visually perceptible. Reference is made here to the Ionic columns of the Ilissus triclinium, while the telamones that frame the existing west window are reminiscent of the Agrigentum sketches by both Klenze and Cockerell. Seen against the evening light pouring through the large window, the sinuous line of the human body offers a contraposto to the rhythmic play of the fluted columns. In the performance of practical purpose we have encouraged, in both rooms, comfort and beauty to arise out of constructional propriety.

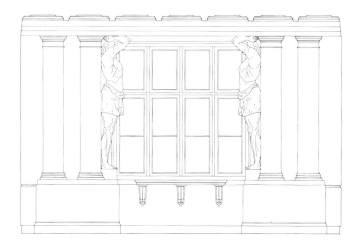

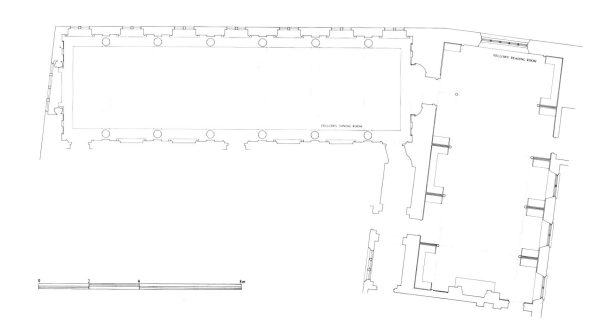

Transversal and

Longitudinal Part Sections

of Fellows'

Dining Room

and

Floor Plan

of the

two rooms

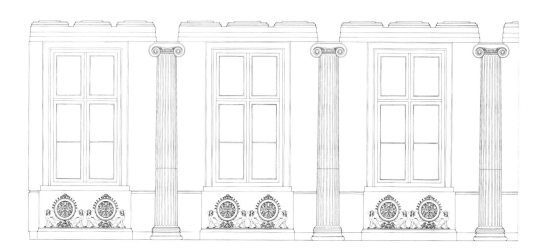

TRANSVERSAL AND

LONGITUDINAL PART SECTIONS

AND

PERSPECTIVE VIEW

OF FELLOWS'

READING ROOM

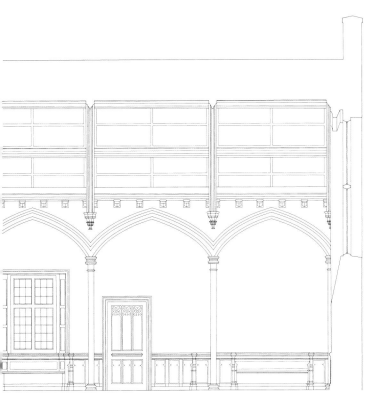

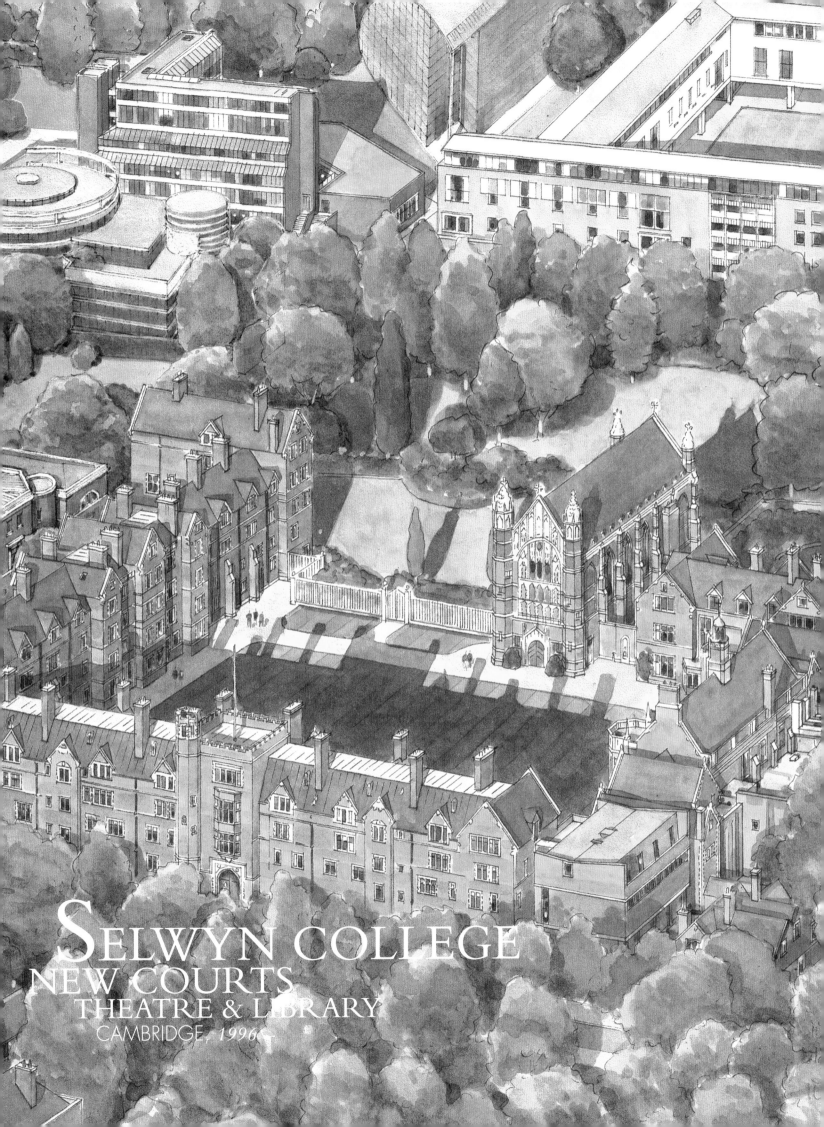

# Selwyn College
## New Courts
### Theatre & Library
#### Cambridge, 1996

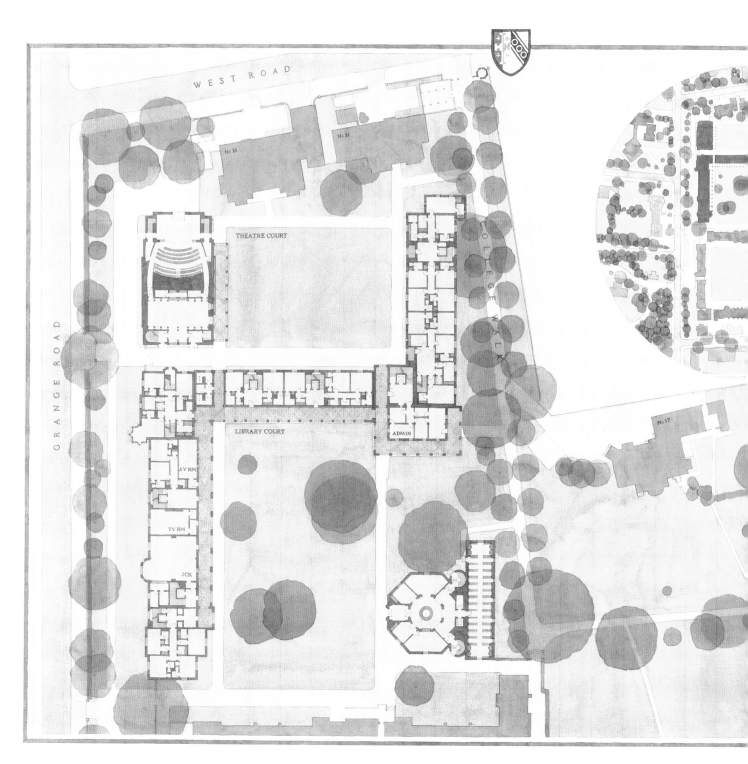

N COLLEGE, CAMBRIDGE
OPOSED MASTERPLAN

PHYRIOS ASSOCIATES

T his is the winning entry in an
invited architectural competition
for a major building programme by
Selwyn College, Cambridge. The
scheme comprises residential accommodation for students and fellows, new
administration facilities, a college library
and auditorium. The new buildings are
organised around a series of traditional
collegiate courts. The courts give a sense
of intimate college community while
fostering leadership within a framework
of shared principles and values. The
masterplan refutes the modernist ten-
dency of designing a college as a mere
'office park' and instead it features a
number of buildings, varied in scale and
character, which interlace with the
existing nineteenth-century buildings
and gardens. We must recognise that the
size of a building must not be determined by the size of the commission.
This is, of course, self-evident yet quite
often today gigantism prevails. We must
recognise that buildings are finite, their
size and scale always defined by the

GRANGE ROAD COMPOSITE ELEVATION SHOWING:

West Elevation of

Grange Road

Range

Left, the Auditorium; Centre, Student Accommodation; Right, Existing Buildings of the Old Court

*nature of their urban typology. In contrast to current modernist planning with its emphasis on machine-like object buildings designed in isolation from both place and history, our proposal for Selwyn College demonstrates an interest in the uniqueness of place and culture and in the continuity of urban form. At Selwyn College the new library, administration building and auditorium are composed into small figural buildings. Around them, as background texture, the residential buildings form and are formed by the two new courts, displaying continuity with the buildings of the existing Old Court while their overall massing offers the enjoyment of a rich and varied composition. Their solid, beautiful and civil materials will weather and mature with usage and time. Their architecture makes reference to the existing Old Court buildings of Selwyn College, but also to the wider context of Cambridge and the great humanist tradition of its collegiate architecture.*

SECTIONAL ELEVATION OF LIBRARY COURT WITH ACCOMMODATION AND ADMINISTRATION BUILDINGS

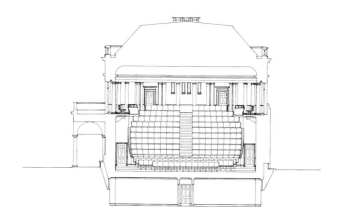

TRANSVERSAL AND LONGITUDINAL SECTION OF THE AUDITORIUM

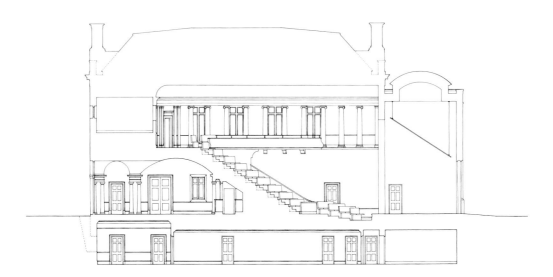

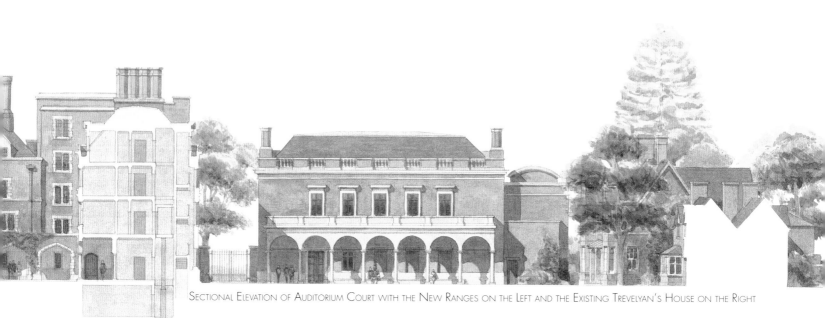

SECTIONAL ELEVATION OF AUDITORIUM COURT WITH THE NEW RANGES ON THE LEFT AND THE EXISTING TREVELYAN'S HOUSE ON THE RIGHT

SECTION OF LIBRARY

EAST ELEVATION OF

GRANGE ROAD

RANGE

COMPOSITE SECTIONAL ELEVATION SHOWING: LEFT, EXISTING OLD COURT; CENTRE, STUDENT ACCOMMODATION; RIGHT, AUDITORIUM

# RESIDENCE
## IN AMMAN
*1996*

F*or centuries the Kingdom of Jordan had been a cross-roads of civilisations. It was the traditions of the Nabateans and of Hellenistic antiquity, however, that Moslem culture later redefined and made its own. This large residence, just outside Amman – the Hellenistic city of Philadelphia of the Decapolis – straddles the crest of a wooded hillside enjoying magnificent views in all directions. The house develops in an additive manner with localised courts and its form is largely governed by the requirement for providing views, natural ventilation and for modulating the strong sunlight of the region. The ground floor comprises a series of reception rooms with an office suite and ancillary service accommodation at opposite ends of the house. Private living quarters and bedroom suites are located at first floor level with terraces and balconies affording views across the surrounding hills. The abundance of good building stone and the long tradition of local stone masonry made it natural to build the residence in load-bearing stone. The Kabatia lime-stone contrasts with the timber pergolas, musharabiyas, iwans and kiosks used traditionally for the passive control of light, temperature and humidity. Much of the detailing has its origin in Moslem architecture and, being concentrated on a capital, a niche or a cornice, it is highly disciplined and in contrast to the smooth stone surfaces of the cubic volumes of the house. Ulti-mately the effect of the architecture is calm simplicity.*

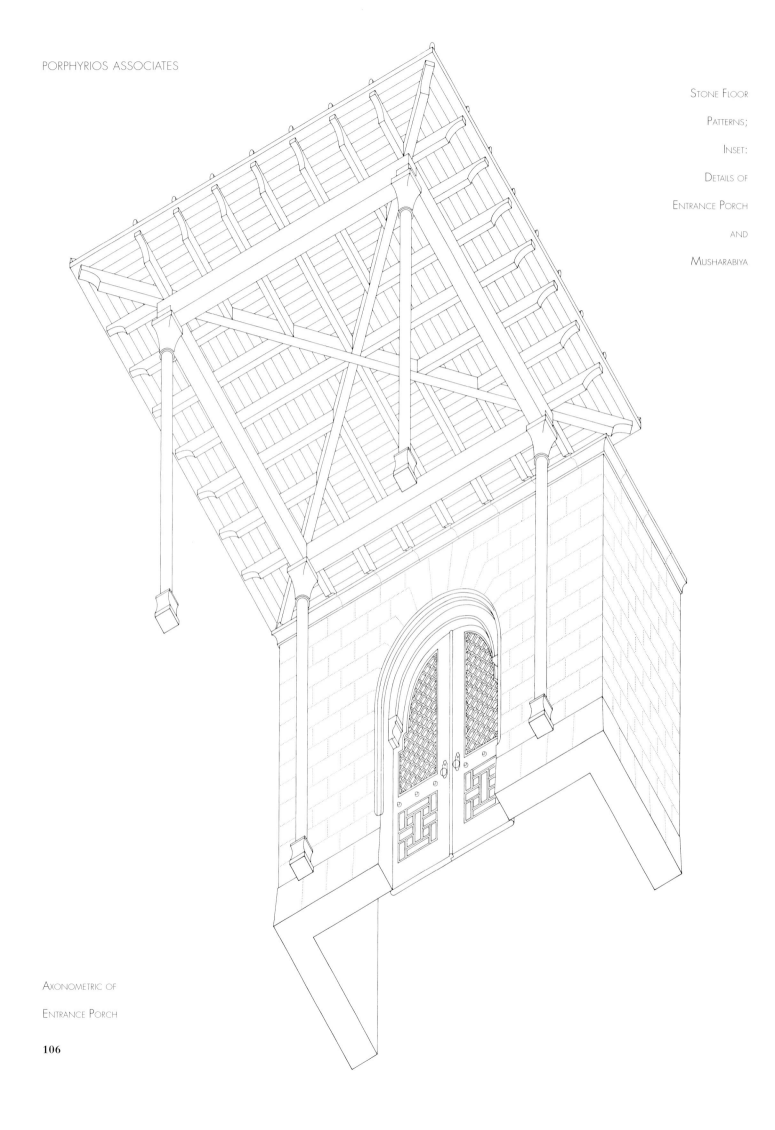

STONE FLOOR

PATTERNS;

INSET:

DETAILS OF

ENTRANCE PORCH

AND

MUSHARABIYA

AXONOMETRIC OF

ENTRANCE PORCH

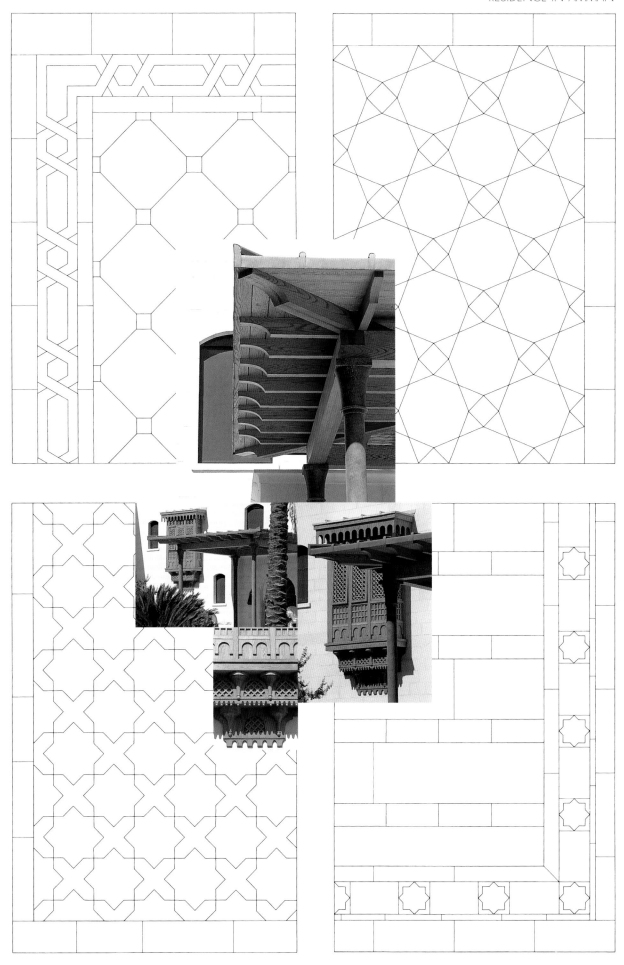

DETAILS OF
LIBRARY LOGGIA
AND
METALWORK;
OVERLEAF:
VIEW
OF THE
SECOND COURT

THE SECOND COURT:

DETAILS

OF THE

PERGOLA AND

TOWER

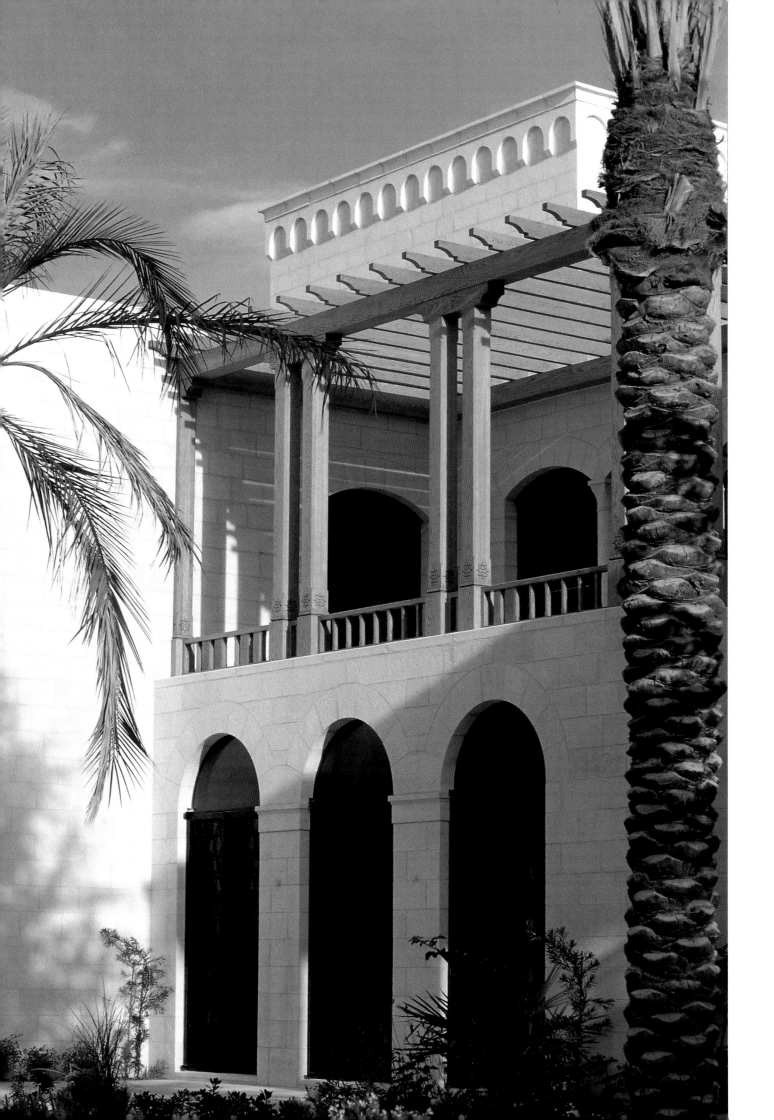

DETAILS

OF THE

PERGOLA,

TOWER AND

CHIMNEY

The Iwan of the Third Court

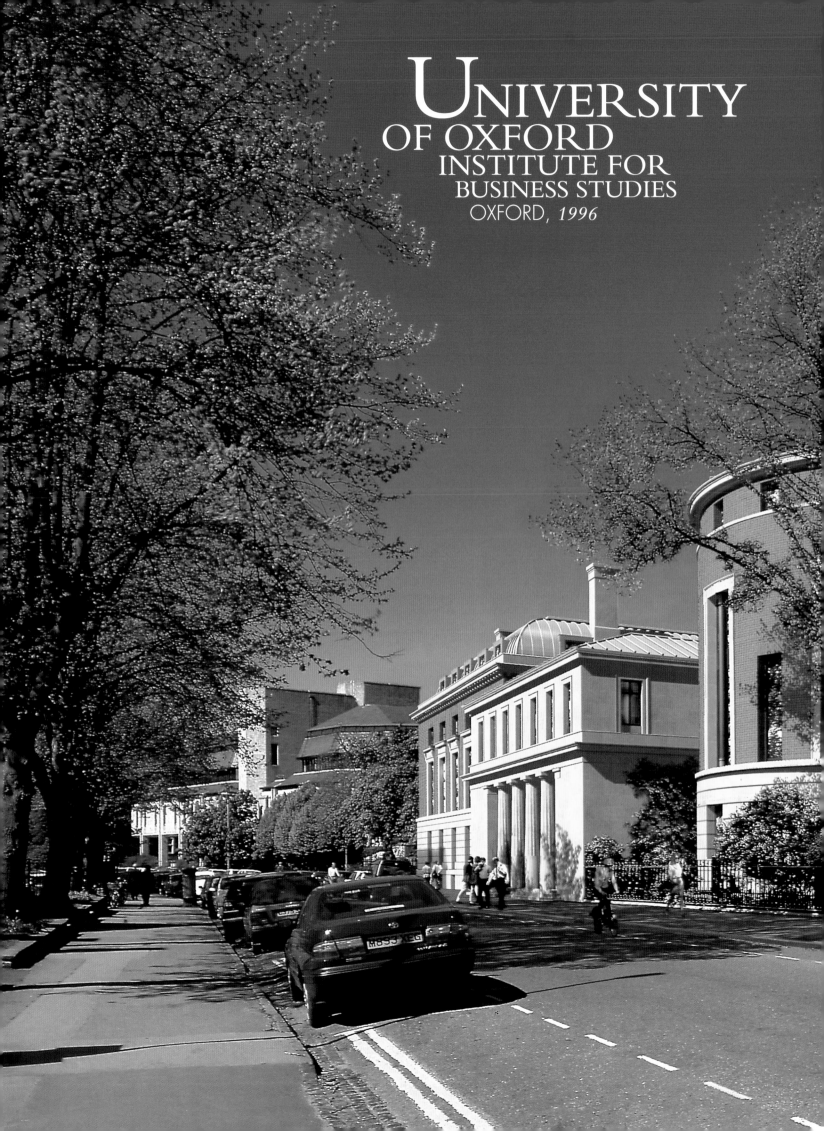

# UNIVERSITY
## OF OXFORD
### INSTITUTE FOR
### BUSINESS STUDIES
OXFORD, *1996*

PERSPECTIVE VIEW OF THE QUADRANGLE SHOWING: LEFT, STUDENT ROTUNDA; CENTRE, ENTRANCE PAVILION; RIGHT, LIBRARY AND ROSTRUM

T*his is an invited competition for the new Institute for Business Studies of the University of Oxford. Our reference has been the Asclepeion of Pergamon, that great Hellenistic complex of buildings which was at the same time architecture and urban design. A stoa defines the three sides of a quadrangle around which are the seminar rooms, lecture theatres, the library and faculty and administration offices. On the fourth side are the entrance pavilion, the rotunda with the student common rooms and the faculty pavilion. Together with the library these three buildings address both the quadrangle and Mansfield Road, thereby representing the Institute as a 'Pantechneion' for business studies. A circular pavilion serves as an open-air rostrum for festive occasions or public debates. Our overall design stresses the use of passive environmental control where buildings are generally in heavyweight materials producing low-response envelopes and with their section assisting with up-flow ventilation. The scheme adopts the Oxford quadrangle as an organisational field while establishing hierarchies between 'figural' and 'background' buildings thus offering identity within a mutually supportive environment.*

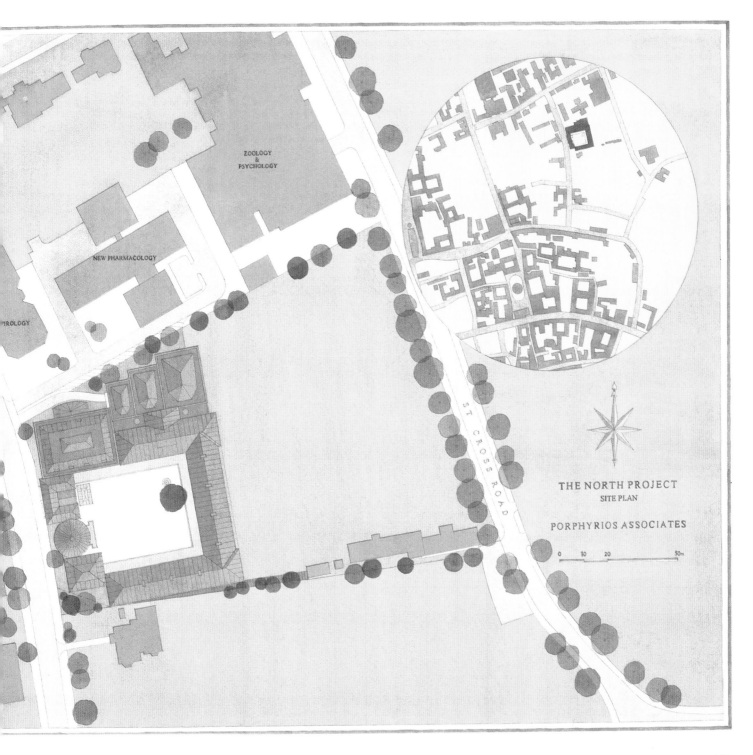

ZOOLOGY
&
PSYCHOLOGY

NEW PHARMACOLOGY

VIROLOGY

ST CROSS ROAD

THE NORTH PROJECT
SITE PLAN

PORPHYRIOS ASSOCIATES

0    10    20              50m

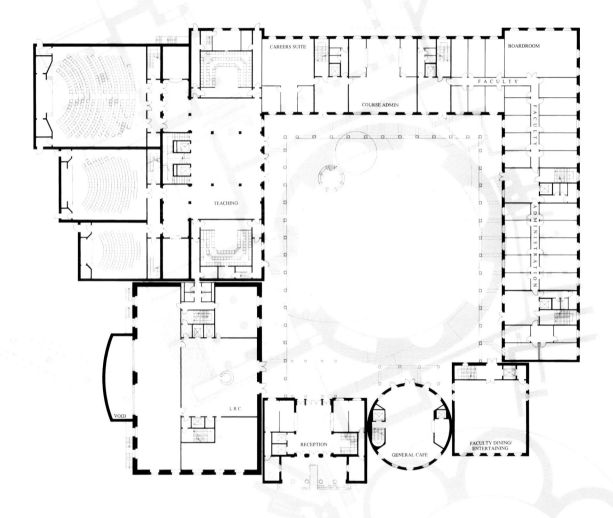

OPPOSITE:

GROUND FLOOR

PLAN

PERSPECTIVE VIEW OF QUADRANGLE

FRONT ELEVATION SHOWING: LEFT, LIBRARY; CENTRE, ENTRANCE PAVILION; RIGHT, STUDENT ROTUNDA AND FACULTY PAVILION

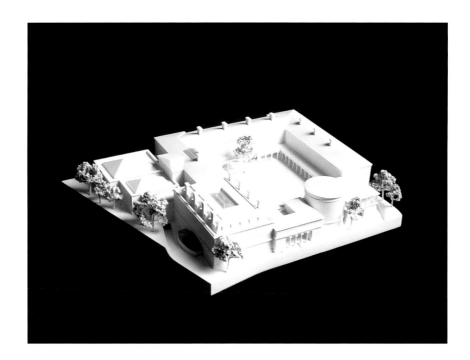

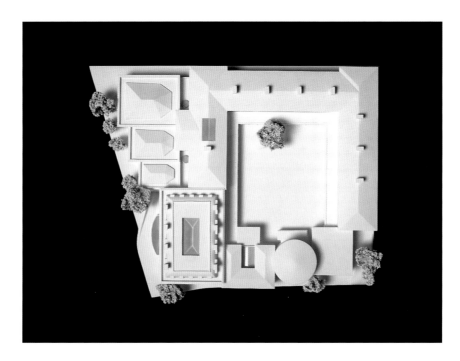

Perspective View of the Student Rotunda and Entrance Pavilion

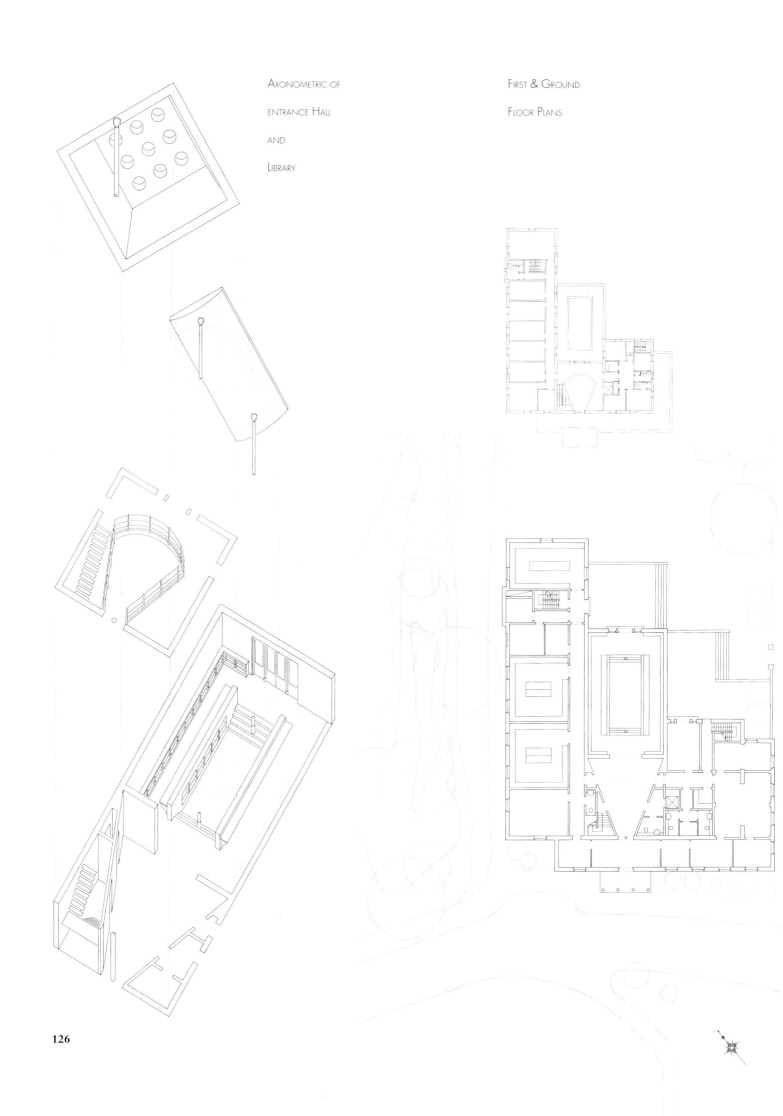

Axonometric of
entrance Hall
and
Library

First & Ground
Floor Plans

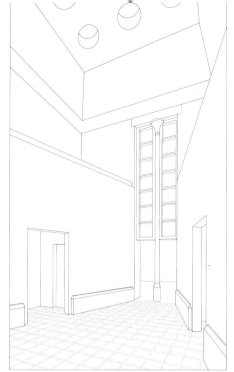

# SANE
## RESEARCH CENTRE
### WARNEFORD HOSPITAL
OXFORD, 1997

A t the site of Warneford Hospital in Oxford, SANE, the organisation for schizophrenia, will establish the Prince of Wales's International Research Centre. The Centre comprises research laboratories, interview rooms, offices and administration, as well as a library that functions also as seminar and lecture hall. The entrance hall has a triangular plan with a double-height skylit cubic volume above. It offers an unsettling experience suggesting, perhaps, that the mind does not simply translate criteria into judgement but that it masters the world by dwelling on the meeting point of competing value systems. The library, grounded as it is by the submerged seminar area, pays homage to the Viipuri library of Aalto. It is lit from above and its convex roof appears to hover on two slender colonnettes. The Centre faces the hospital buildings while its L-shape plan opens up freely towards the 'gardens of contemplation' which form part of the medical programme for patients.

FIGURE-GROUND PLAN SHOWING THE CENTRE IN CONTEXT

200    100    50    25    0    25    50    100    200

127

# WINDSOR RESORT

HURGHADA, *1994*

Our proposal is for a small resort town which meets the requirements of the programme while providing the site with a mix of functions and centres of activity. An open-air theatre, the timber canopy of the market square, the coffee pavilion of the palm square as well as the numerous shops and restaurants of the main square, all define a multi-use and varied

system of public spaces around which hotel accommodation and offices are interwoven. The polygonal lighthouse, dramatically overlooking the beach, houses a diving centre and a small marina for the boats that take visitors for excursions to the coral reefs in the Red Sea.

# MAGDALEN
## SQUASH COURTS
### CENTRE
#### OXFORD, *1994*

Located outside the walls of the College, the squash courts centre for Magdalen College, Oxford, is a short distance along Addison Walk. The building serves also as an entrance pavilion to a small annex of the College that is set amongst rural surroundings beside Holywell Ford and the River Cherwell. Conceived as a sports club, it comprises three squash courts with the necessary changing facilities and viewing galleries. The courts are arranged in an additive manner around the rotunda of the staircase and from the galleries one can also have spectacular views of the deer park and the College buildings beyond. Reclaimed bricks, local stone dressings and stained oak timberwork are used in their robust, unadorned state to reflect the building's rural setting.

VIEW

SHOWING

ENTRANCE ROTUNDA

AND

GLAZED

VIEWING GALLERY

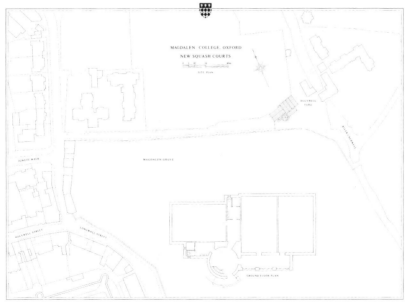

VIEW

FROM

THE SOUTH

GROUND FLOOR

PLAN

AND

LOCATION

PLAN

AXONOMETRIC

SHOWING

THE SQUASH COURTS,

THE VIEWING GALLERIES

AND THE ROTUNDA

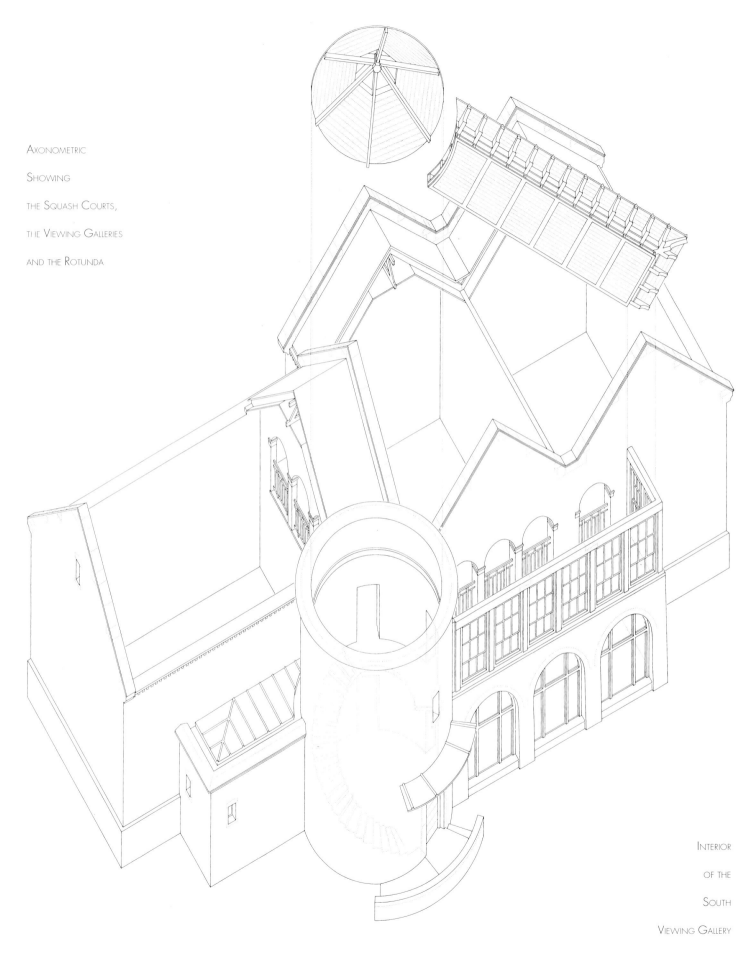

INTERIOR

OF THE

SOUTH

VIEWING GALLERY

INTERIOR VIEW

OF

TYPICAL

SQUASH COURT

INTERIOR VIEW

OF THE

GROUND FLOOR

GALLERY

INTERIOR VIEW

OF THE

ROTUNDA

# ALLATINI
## MASTERPLAN
SALONICA, *1996*

PREVIOUS PAGES:

PERSPECTIVE VIEW

OF THE

NEW ALLATINI SQUARE

WITH THE

GREAT CHIMNEY

OF THE

19TH-CENTURY

FACTORY

PERSPECTIVE VIEWS OF THE NEW NORTH AND SOUTH SQUARES

W hen the Allatini flour mills were relocated outside the city of Salonica, the buildings of the nineteenth-century factory were consigned to the slow destruction of time. Over the years, many proposals have been drawn up for developing the derelict site, all in a modernist idiom of steel and glass. Our masterplan, instead, preserves the existing factory buildings and adds new ones creating a rich urban fabric with a distinct neo-classical character. Adjacent to the Great Chimney, the old mills and silos are converted to an Intercontinental Hotel which presides over the new central square and enjoys splendid views to the south towards the bay of Salonica. Other listed buildings are converted into offices or galleries as suggested by their spatial organisation, while the new buildings are developed speculatively in line with our masterplan and are designed by different architects to house shops, offices and housing. Pedestrian access to the underground car park is through a number of pavilions in the squares, thus safeguarding against the design of an insular megastructure. This is not a 'gated' development but a mixed-use neighbourhood which extends the streets, the open green spaces and the squares of the city of Salonica into a richly varied urban culture to be enjoyed by all. Allatini is the first project of this magnitude in Greece to adopt a traditional masterplan which, both by its urban and architectural design, places great emphasis on the modernising value of tradition.

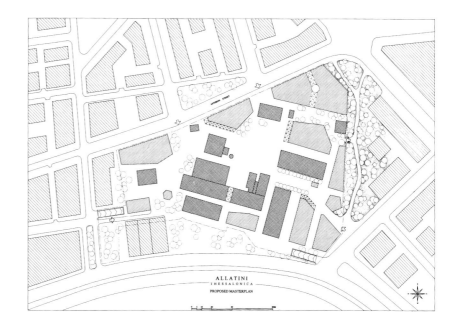

ALLATINI
THESSALONICA
PROPOSED MASTERPLAN

PERSPECTIVE VIEW

OF THE

PARTERRES

WITH THE

OVAL SQUARE

IN THE

BACKGROUND

# KINGSTON MILLS
## MASTERPLAN
### BRADFORD ON AVON, *1996*

GENERAL

MASTERPLAN

*When the factory of Kingston Mills closed, the site lay
derelict along the banks of the river Avon, next to its
fourteenth-century bridge, in the centre of the picturesque town
of Bradford on Avon in Wiltshire. We felt strongly that this
beautiful site should not become yet another hyper-market, an
'office park' or a suburban volume housing development: easy
profitable options which would, however, stifle the town with*

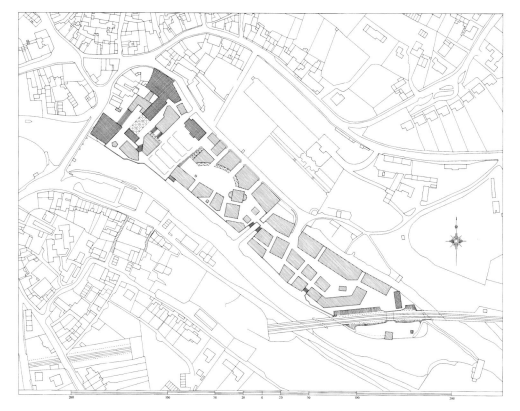

*their mono-functional use and vast car park requirements. Our
scheme is for a mixed use development of small shops and
offices, leisure buildings and galleries, a small hotel, workshops,
housing and graduate student accommodation; all in one- to
three-storey buildings interwoven with streets, squares and with
a public corniche along the banks of the river Avon.*

# Wadi Rum
## FORT HOTEL
WADI RUM, *1995*

Among other points of view about tourism today is the environmental ethics perspective which addresses ecological conservation by way of land stewardship, the preservation of biodiversity, and the insistence that nature possesses intrinsic value. Wadi Rum is an ancient river valley in southern Jordan, amidst mountains of red sandstone rising several thousand feet above a vast desert landscape.

"Landscape in childhood's dreams was never so vast and silent. We were ashamed to flaunt our smallness in the presence of the stupendous hills," wrote T. E. Lawrence about Wadi Rum.  In consultation with the authorities we were asked to design a hotel but we proposed an encampment.  The site is near the Al Makhman Canyon where a large dune rises from the bed of the Wadi to a height of about fifteen metres.  Our proposed Qasr Wadi Rum occupies the highest point on the dune and it takes the form of a desert castle or Qasr, reminiscent of the eighth-century desert residences for the semi-nomadic Umayyad caliphs. The site is organised into three main terraces with living accommodation incorporated into the massive perimeter stone walls.  Public functions such as shops, restaurants, administration, baths, and the large shaded iwans all comprise free-standing buildings sited variously on the terraces amidst lush planting and pools.  Passively controlled ventilation and cooling, solar power and recycling are utilised to reduce waste and energy requirements.

LOCATION PLAN AND GROUND FLOOR PLAN

AERIAL PERSPECTIVE VIEW

OPPOSITE:

AERIAL PHOTOGRAPH OF THE WADI

PREVIOUS SPREAD:

VIEW OF THE WADI WITH THE QASR ON THE LEFT

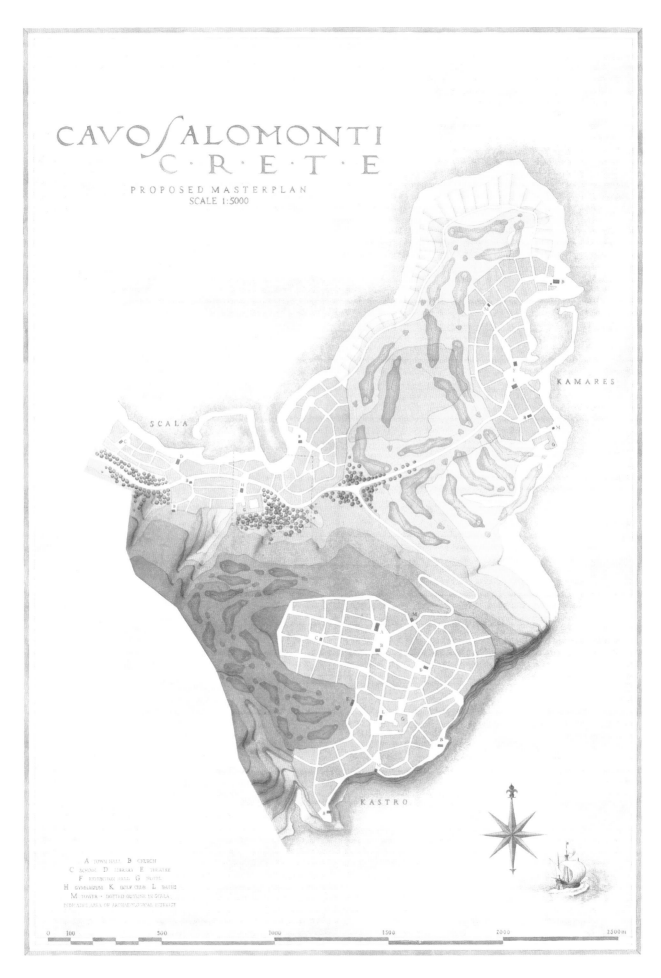

# CAVO SALOMONTI
## C·R·E·T·E

PROPOSED MASTERPLAN
SCALE 1:5000

KAMARES

SCALA

KASTRO

A TOWN HALL   B CHURCH
C SCHOOL  D LIBRARY  E THEATRE
F EXHIBITION HALL  G HOTEL
H GYMNASIUM  K GOLF CLUB  L BATHS
M TOWER • DOTTED OUTLINE IN SCALA
INDICATES AREA OF ARCHAEOLOGICAL INTEREST

0   100          500          1000          1500          2000          2500 m

# CAVO SALOMONTI
# MASTERPLAN
## CRETE, *1996*

Imagine it has been sunny outside for months, a sea of dazzling clarity forming the horizon, the rugged landscape mixed with thyme, rock-honey and a few olive trees. Cavo Salomonti is a 350-hectare peninsula at the easternmost tip of the island of Crete. When we were first asked to prepare designs for the masterplan we insisted that the landscape must stay intact with all development concentrated in three settlements planned in the manner of traditional local villages. The new coastal towns of Scala and Kamares are sited along the seashore, around natural rocky bays, while Kastro is perched high on the hill enjoying splendid views of the whole peninsula and of the sea beyond. Scala is knitted into an ancient archaeological site and it serves as the main harbour for fishing boats, commercial ferries and cruise ships. Kamares develops radially around a marina with a public square at the water's edge where boats are pulled ashore for repair. All three towns are planned along traditional principles where houses, shops, churches and community buildings all interweave with streets, promenades, squares and gardens to create a functional and pleasing framework for daily life. The buildings are neoclassical or vernacular in character, of two and three storeys and most have their own small private gardens, rich with lemon and almond trees and with the slender cypresses rising everywhere.

OVERLEAF:

PERSPECTIVE VIEW

OF SCALA

WITH KASTRO

IN THE

BACKGROUND

PERSPECTIVE VIEW OF KASTRO

# THREE BRINDLEYPLACE
## OFFICE BUILDING
BIRMINGHAM, *1995*

Brindleyplace is a masterplanned, mixed-use development in the city of Birmingham with office buildings, shops, restaurants, housing, leisure buildings and with the Oozells Street School restored as a gallery. Designed by different architects, the buildings follow the masterplan which produces an urban pattern of streets converging around two public squares and the canal front. Three Brindleyplace is the office building we have designed. Its massing is additive: it presents a civic front on the side of the square and steps down to three storeys towards the canal. The tower rises as if embedded within the urban block and serves as a landmark for the entire Brindleyplace development. The main entrance leads through a double-height arcade into a lofty foyer, which in turn opens onto the central seven-storey glazed atrium. The atrium is the very heart of the building revealing at once its organisation in plan and section. It has an ashlar stone base with an arcade at ground floor, a columniated middle, and a top loggia surmounted by the glazed roof. The aim here has been to project a light post-and-spandrel structure in contrast to the solidity of the external masonry, thereby revealing the two constructional principles of bearing wall masonry and steel frame structure at work. At each office level, lifts open onto broad balconies overlooking the atrium. The 13 metre floor plate and 2.7 metre floor-to-ceiling height provide excellent working conditions with ample natural light and the potential for natural ventilation. The building has a steel frame with external walls

*in self-supporting brick and ashlar stone construction. All architectural projections and rusticated surfaces are in reconstituted stone. Windows are detailed in metal and roofs are in terne-coated steel sheeting. Generally elevations are organised into three sections: a rusticated base, a middle and an attic floor. Cornices, window surrounds and string courses all lend the building a sculptural character, ornamental profiles underline its constructional reading, while motifs like anthemia, reeds, roundels and acroteria are used as punctuation devices or to soften the skyline. Along the elevation to the main square the interweaving of the arcade arches imparts a pictorial depth to the plane of the wall, with half-round relieving arches transferring the weight onto piers and quarter engaged Doric columns. Thus a figure-ground dialogue emerges: from a structural viewpoint, the half-round arch is the figure, whilst the pointed arch becomes a figure only on account of the resultant void. This constant oscillation in the reading of figure-ground is heightened further by the memory of the trabeated system to which the Doric columns allude. Here, where the building addresses the public square, the history of western structural traditions is narrated in stone.*

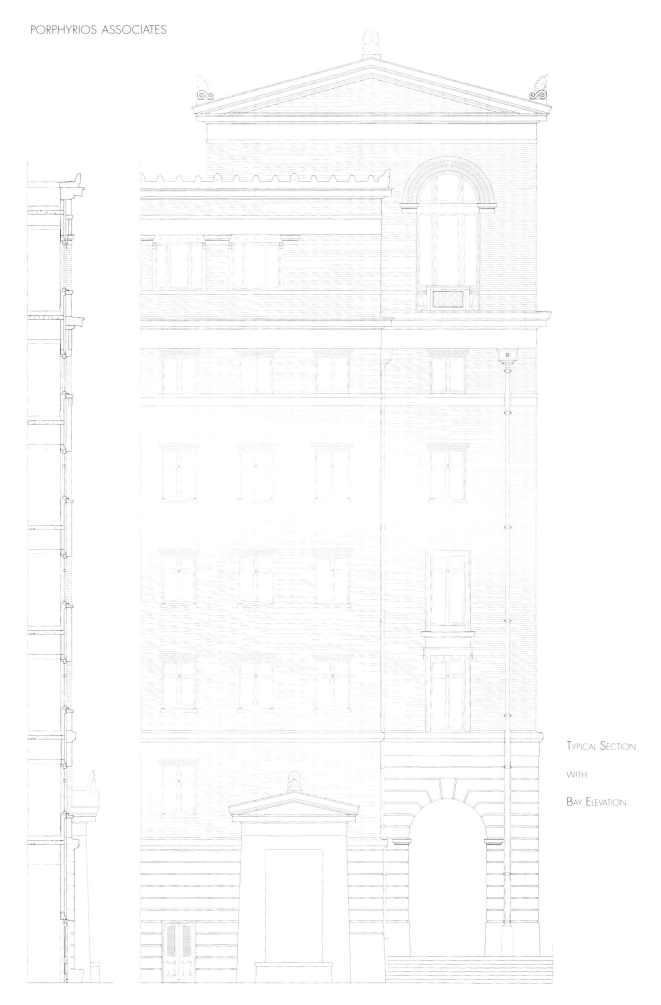

TYPICAL SECTION

WITH

BAY ELEVATION

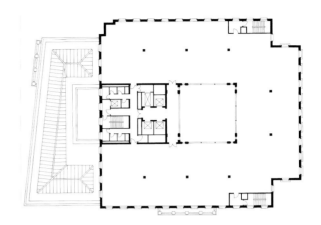

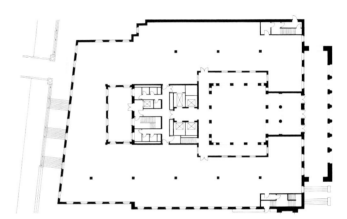

TYPICAL

AND

GROUND

FLOOR PLANS

FIGURE-GROUND

PLAN

SHOWING THE

BRINDLEYPLACE

DEVELOPMENT

IN CONTEXT

Perspective

View of

Atrium

and View

of Atrium

as Built

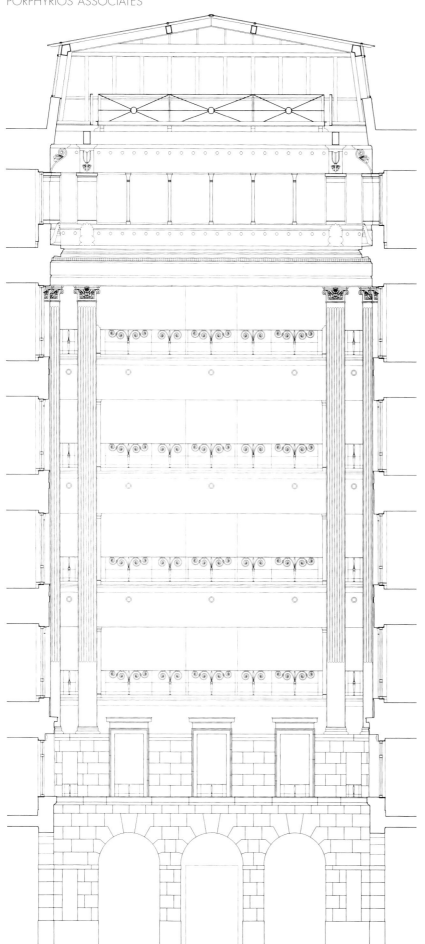

SECTION OF
ATRIUM AND
DETAIL VIEW
OF THE
FIFTH AND
SIXTH FLOORS

The Arcaded

Entrance

The Doric

Colonnade

Detail View

from the

Square

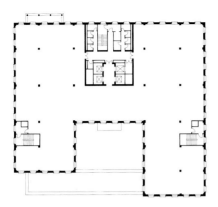

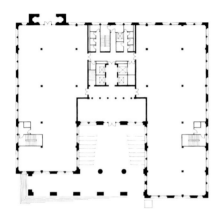

FIGURE-GROUND

PLAN

SHOWING THE

BRINDLEYPLACE

DEVELOPMENT

IN CONTEXT

*S even Brindleyplace forms and is formed by the two adjacent squares. Its location suggested a composite building that is both figure and ground, displaying continuity with the urban fabric yet with a distinct figural presence. Its massing is subtractive: an incomplete courtyard building inflects towards the main square. A few steps and the arcade describe a podium that reconstructs the archaeology of the building's plan. On the side of the smaller square, a projecting volume steps onto the pavement announcing the building while holding the corner. The top storey together with the windows and the terminating cornice are all detailed in metal. Brick, steel, aluminium and stone are here brought together with a calm attentiveness to the manner of their co-option.*

# SEVEN BRINDLEYPLACE
## OFFICE BUILDING
BIRMINGHAM, *1997*

Elevation

Facing

the Main

Square

# WINDSOR
## RAS-NASRANI
### RESORT
SHARM EL-SHEIKH, *1995*

The role that the powerful force of world tourism can play in improving sustainable development in ecologically fragile regions is today one of the key issues for policy-makers and governments. We must call into doubt the complacency vis-à-vis present environmental degradation. Traditional models of tourist development in the form of towns and villages, rather than modernist megabuildings, can provide a basis sufficient for sustainable development to become a reality.  Our proposal takes the form of a traditional walled seaside town, similar to those found on the Alexandrian coast and along the Nile in Lower Egypt. The aim is to create an urban fabric of squares, streets and urban blocks which will provide a varied and responsive environment.  A number of distinct centres of activity are organised around four main squares and the corniche along the south-east wall of the town. This perimeter stone wall enclosing the town defines its limits and safeguards against indiscriminate sprawl and the consequent spoiling of the sea front, the adjoining desert and the hills beyond.  Resort accommodation is here in the form of row houses, semi-detached houses and free-standing villas, all set within landscaped urban blocks defined by low stone walls.  By avoiding multi-storey structures and reducing mechanical and air-conditioning services – which a conventional hotel complex would have otherwise required – we generated a budget sufficient for the construction of the houses, shops and restaurants and of the open public spaces of the town.

PERSPECTIVE

VIEWS OF

ROW HOUSES

AND

SEMI-DETACHED

VILLAS

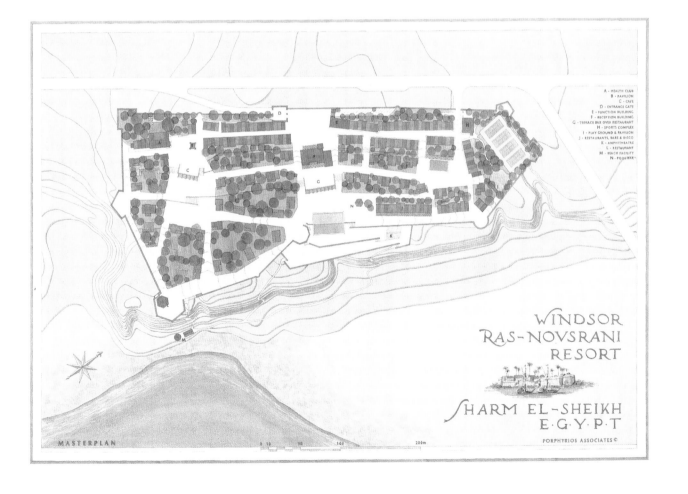

A - HEALTH CLUB
B - PAVILION
C - CAFE
D - ENTRANCE GATE
E - FUNCTION BUILDING
F - RECEPTION BUILDING
G - TERRACE BAR OVER RESTAURANT
H - SPORTS COMPLEX
I - PLAY GROUND & PAVILION
J - RESTAURANTS, BARS & DISCO
K - AMPHITHEATRE
L - RESTAURANT
M - BEACH FACILITY
N - POOL BAR

WINDSOR
RAS-NOVSRANI
RESORT

SHARM EL-SHEIKH
E·G·Y·P·T

PORPHYRIOS ASSOCIATES©

MASTERPLAN

COMPOSITE
ELEVATION
OF THE
TOWN
FROM THE
RED SEA

# THE DAKIS JOANNOU
## COLLECTION
### GALLERIES
ATHENS, *1996*

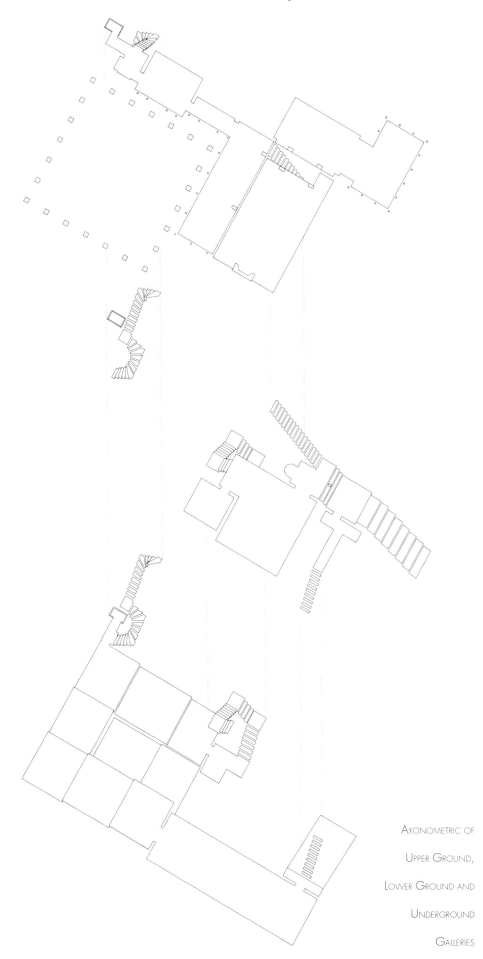

With some three hundred modern paintings and sculptures dating from the mid-80s onwards – including works by Katharina Fritsch, Robert Gober, Mike Kelly, Jeff Koons and Kiki Smith – the Dakis Joannou Collection is one of Europe's leading private collections of contemporary art. Its Athens gallery, a large 60s' villa set on a hillside north of the city centre has grown over the years in an additive manner. The strategy was to form a new setting for its varied volumes with the creation of a new open court, defined by a perimeter colonnade and with the new galleries located underground. Upon entering the underground galleries, the visitor traverses a drawbridge, suggestive perhaps of the play between the real and fictive in art, while the sense of passage is heightened by the light that filters through the underwater windows of the pool. The largest gallery has a flat ceiling with a glazed oculus but the floor is stepped in a helicoidal manner, like an inverted ziggurat – reminiscent of the descending staircases in Piranesi's Carceri. The floors of the galleries are in Pentelicon marble while the walls and ceilings, all made of plasterboard, are ephemeral elements that change according to the requirements of the exhibits. Solid, traditional materials that will age are juxtaposed with industrial, modern materials that perish, making reference to the nature of the brief.

AXONOMETRIC OF

UPPER GROUND,

LOWER GROUND AND

UNDERGROUND

GALLERIES

VIEW OF
UPPER GROUND
GALLERY
AND
DETAIL VIEW
OF THE
THIRD
UNDERGROUND
GALLERY

PREVIOUS SPREAD:

VIEW

OF THE

THIRD

UNDERGROUND

GALLERY

VIEW

OF THE

FIRST

UNDERGROUND

GALLERY WITH

DRAWBRIDGE

VIEW

OF THE

SECOND

UNDERGROUND

GALLERY

VIEW OF THE

UPPER GROUND

GALLERY

AND

DETAIL VIEW

OF THE

THIRD

UNDERGROUND

GALLERY

# HIGH-TECH
## AND SUCH MISNOMERS
### DEMETRI PORPHYRIOS

It is said that Proust knew *Praeterita* by heart. Given the length of the book, the claim seems improbable yet one can see why it is made. Proust admired Ruskin "for speaking of what [gave him] joy to remember." At the same time Proust saw in Ruskin the last elegiac masterbuilder who must have felt that "the art of building is drawing to an end because the epic side of construction is dying out."

Traditional construction – and its epic dimension in tectonics – always invoked a potential order that derived from the form-giving capacity of the material used. Tectonics, as the *techne* of construction delineated the ontological experience of construction. The concern of tectonics has always been threefold. First, the nature and formal properties of construction materials, be they timber, brick, stone, iron, etc. Second, the procedures of jointing, in other words the way that elements of construction are put together. Thirdly, the visual statics of form, that is the way by which the eye is satisfied about stability, unity and balance and their variations or opposites.

This means that in any encounter with traditional building it is not the particular exigencies of construction but, rather, the experience of tectonics that is brought to bear. Tectonics stands as the highest fulfilment of all construction. It makes construction speak out in the sense of revealing the ontology of constructing.

It is this very 'revealing of the ontology of constructing' that modernist technology cancels out and annuls. Consider, for example, a panelised brick wall: its bond, coursing and the properties of its mortar do not allow for a uniform distribution of expansion – as would be the case in

POST

AND LINTEL

TECTONICS

IN SELINUNTE

traditional brickwork. Instead, all expansion is concentrated in the movement joint. The result is an inert panel that bears only visual vestiges of traditional brick construction. Upon failure it falls out as a disembodied panel leaving behind it the frame onto which it was propped and a plethora of damp-proof membranes and insulating quilts. To be repaired it requires shop fabrication, most probably by a manufacturer that has already gone into liquidation, thereby implicating the client, the architect and the contractor in a lengthy and costly lawsuit.

Building technology is today commodified. It promises to bring the forces of nature and culture under control and liberate us from the misery of toil. The promise of liberation takes the form of conspicuous availability. Building materials are 'available' off the shelf and their procurement imposes no burden on us. Concrete, sawn timber, mild and stainless steel, hermetically sealed glazing, PVC panels, extruded aluminium, insulating plasterboards, rubber gaskets and numerous sealants, etc., are all at the tip of our fingers. We only have to fill an order form and check that the product has an Agrément Certificate.

Designers and contractors alike are removed from the craft of building and consequently from an empirical understanding of the properties and behaviour of the materials they are specifying. Building materials have become mere technological products. What I mean here is that they make no demand on our skill, knowledge or attention. Their properties, functioning, constructional behaviour, the 'what-a-brick-wants-to-be' quality that Kahn has spoken of so eloquently, are all today concealed. This concealment is the *sine qua non* of commodified technology. Consider the commodity in the following examples: in the case of the radiator it is warmth; a swipe card provides access; and an air-conditioning unit furnishes environmental comfort. In using these products we are interested exclusively in the commodity furnished. As a rule we are not required to know how they work or how they are made or maintained. In fact the less troubled we are about such questions the more valuable the commodity offered. Should a problem arise, a distinct body of 'specialists' is empowered with the necessary know-how and we can buy their service with a cheque or through an insurance agreement.

This reminds me of Vaucanson's mechanical duck that flapped its wings, drank, ate and evacuated, becoming a most celebrated attraction in mid eighteenth-century London. People crowded to see this remarkable fowl yet nobody bothered to ask about its inner workings. Its value resided in the spectacle the automaton offered. Vaucanson's duck made no demand on the skill, knowledge or attention of the enthusiastic spectators.

My intention here, of course, is not to denigrate technology – far from it. I rather want to look at the implications of the recent commodification of technology and suggest ways of positive engagement with it.

Let me go back to the example of carpentry. As we know, traditional carpentry requires a deep knowledge of the properties of timber and a sensibility that is sharpened and strengthened in skill. This skill shapes the artisan and forms his character. By contrast, glue-laminated technology disburdens the contractor and the designer of any requirement for skill in carpentry. Similarly, reconstituted stone (a euphemism for blocks of reinforced concrete) releases us from the obligation to understand masonry construction altogether. It is instructive to note that the more off-the-shelf building materials proliferate, the more skill is replaced by incompetence.

Another implication of commodified technology is that of rampant obsolescence. Consider how many of us can repair a fractured sealed glazing unit, a dented aluminium panel, a digital watch or even a dishwasher. This is so since commodities have a built-in factor of obsolescence that demands their replacement and thereby their dissemination. The same thing cannot be said of plaster, masonry, timberwork, metalwork, etc., in short of what are known as traditional materials. Maintenance and repair, in this case, are an integral part of their life-cycle necessitating attention, knowledge and skill. The indispensable qualification 'maintenance free' that graces the marketing brochures of many modern building materials is but a sham. Indeed, frequently if not always, the expression 'maintenance free' means 'non-reparable.'

It is important to remember that when commodified building materials resist our engagement through care, knowledge and skill, then technology leads to human estrange-

ment. When building materials cannot be domesticated but are merely presented as alien fabrications incapable of ageing, they can no longer speak of a particular place and thereby carry no resonance and consequence.

This brings to mind David Billington's distinction between structures and machines. "Structures and Machines" he says, "are related by contrast. Structures are roads, bridges, waterworks [...] and buildings, whereas machines are cars, trains, ships, pumps, television sets, computers, [...] and air-conditioners." Structures are permanent, site specific and are experienced as part of the landscape. Machines are transient, non site-specific and are indifferent to the landscape. In this sense, buildings cannot be confused with machines. To conflate buildings with machines is to mistake the former for mere commodities, thereby stripping them of their ability to register ageing as a positive event that determines new possibilities of meaning.

Buildings have grown up with man, not merely with the circumstances of an age. Our buildings and towns are not expendable 'machines for living' nor are they the monopoly of one particular period. They rise with man and endure with human nature.

The commodification of the building industry in the last fifty years, however, has led to a progressive loss of physical quality in our buildings and in the public spaces of our cities. The critique against the International Style in the 1960s and of post-modernist architecture more recently, is more profound than merely a critique of taste and fashion, for it represents an attempt on the part of the public to avoid the loss of qualitative experience.

This may somewhat surprise us. But we only have to consider the high-tech image of the technical world sold today, from the digital watch to the space-frame. High-tech conjures up the inevitable mirage of progress and fosters the illusion of a society emancipated from history, individual taste and social prejudice. In fact, the problematic relationship between high-tech and humanism is shown today by the systematic and wholesale destruction the former inaugurates: the destruction of craft, of independent workshops, of the versatile ingenuity of traditional technologies; of the immense knowledge regional cultures developed over centuries; of the inventions and skills which have been practised for millennia within a balanced ecological framework; and, not least, of the knowledge and *métier* that skilled labour transmitted from one generation to another.

Instead, the mechanical order that high-tech celebrates is based upon quantitative production in the service of the economic expansion of centralised conglomerates. This mechanical order feeds on totalization: It demands universal conformity to its principles; it institutes artificially programmed choice; it demands the eclipse of the anthropological and the historical; it reinforces docile conformity to industrial products; and it deprives experience of its sensuous, representational dimension. And yet, such a mechanical order is presented today as liberation and progress! But I ask, liberation from what? "Liberation from the conditions under which man has flourished? Liberation from a rewarding relationship with a varied and responsive environment – both human and natural?" (Mumford).

This raises, in my opinion, a crucial question: How can humanist architecture survive in a world marked by an opposition between technological commodification and the yearning for individual cultures that can sustain freedom in public life? To attain a balance between technology and humanism we must cultivate an attitude of engagement and franchisement of technological culture. Our buildings must not alienate us from the character of the land and the mood of the day and seasons. We must resist the intimidation of commodified technology by understanding how its products work, how they are used, maintained and how they can be re-used.

Our aim need not so much be to dissipate the difference between humanist and technological culture, but to challenge the notion that difference implies hostility and an adversarial future. Ultimately, we must construct a social commitment that embraces those aspects of traditional and modern technology which enhance rather than demean our everyday social life.

*The title of this essay arose out of a discussion I had with Nigel Cox a couple of years ago. A version of this essay was first published in* Harvard Design Magazine, *Fall 1997.*

COURTYARD

PERGOLA

ON THE

ISLAND OF CHIOS

COURTYARD

IN PORTUGAL

# RESTORATION
## AND VALUE
### DEMETRI PORPHYRIOS

F ar from withering away, the historical is in our days a congested trade. In literature, criticism, art, architecture, interior decoration, tourism, archaeology, or the auction houses, the value of the 'historical' – cultural and financial – is paramount. There is simply too much of it.

The myth of the historical is prone to over-production, rapid turnover and speedy obsolescence. There is no common measure left between the life of a book, a work of art or a building and the lifespan of the cultural movement that produced and sustained it.

Two examples occupying opposite extremes in our understanding of the historical may help my discussion here. What I have in mind is on one hand the Campanile of St. Mark's and on the other the bas-relief recently discovered at Canford Manor.

Since the eleventh century the Campanile of St. Mark's had taken on a symbolic character that represented Venice herself. The religious, secular and civic values of the republic were all represented in the image of the Campanile and it was this symbolic fortitude that allowed the monument to take hold of experience. When in 1902, therefore, the Campanile fell down, a great debate ensued. Was the disaster to be accepted as the irrevocable consequence of the passing of time consigning the monument to oblivion? Was it incumbent upon the Venetians to restore the Campanile to its former glory? Or was it advisable to organise a competition (like the one recently held following the Windsor Castle fire) in search of a contemporary talent to whom the design of the tower in the 'spirit of the age' would be entrusted?

At the time the Campanile collapsed, the London *Daily Telegraph* took the view that the Campanile had "fallen with all the associations that have clustered around it over the centuries and it may fervently be hoped that no civic zeal for restoration will ever lead the Venetian prefect to try and build it up again … [for] the grace its builders gave it is lost for ever in the art they knew."

The view expressed by the *Daily Telegraph* is, with hindsight, that of a nascent modernism. The Campanile was but a relic of the past "safe upon the canvasses of Canaletto," wrote the newspaper. Its actual building fabric, however, was seen as irretrievable due to an intense suspicion that authentic experience under modern conditions is somehow not available. Once destroyed, historical artefacts lose their rootedness, it was argued, and no restorative scheme can give them back a legitimate life. The history of a ruined monument is unwittingly revealed as a history of disintegration that may afford only aesthetic satisfaction in the form of melancholy nostalgia. It should be left to suffer steady decay consigned to the action of time.

The opposite view, of course, prevailed. The Campanile of Venice was duly and faithfully restored to its previous familiar shape and form. Not interested in the picturesqueness of decay nor troubled by the alleged inauthenticity of construction, the Venetians chose to restore the Campanile in a faithful manner. Soon there seemed to be no scar on the skyline of the laguna. The paramount symbolic significance of the Campanile overrode the intellectual pretentiousness of a nascent modernism.

A different way of approaching the subject of historical value can be seen in the most recent discovery at Canford Manor in southern England. A stone fragment decorating the snack bar of Canford School – hitherto considered but a mere replica cast of a bygone original – turned out to be an authentic stone panel from the Assyrian palace of King Ashurnasirpal II. Examined and authenticated by the British Museum, it fetched $11.9 million at Christie's London auction house making it the most highly valued bas-relief in the world. Surely its value is not historical for it may be safe to assume that its buyer shares nothing with the civic ideals of the Assyrian kingdom nor with the artistic canons of its sculptor. Its value must rest elsewhere: on the rarity and age-value of the artefact which render the bas-relief priceless by removing it from the nexus of commodification. To possess such an inimitable bas-relief is to strip it of its commodity character conferring on it a fancier's value. Singularity and age-value converge here to produce the idea of the authentic. Age-value and rarity are here in direct contrast with the historical value we encountered in the case of the Campanile.

In his essay 'The modern Cult of Monuments,' written only a year after the collapse of the Venice Campanile, the Viennese art historian Alois Riegl gives an account of the cultural preoccupations surrounding the idea of the monument. Riegl distinguishes between the ideas of *use-value*, *age-value*, and *historical value*.

*Use-value* refers to the concrete, practical requirements of material life. "An antique building still in use," Riegl writes, "must be maintained in such a condition that it can accommodate people without endangering life or health." Thus it must be repaired anew irrespective of whether the new stones or timbers may be authentic. A building which is still in use mitigates against its imprisonment as an open-air museum. Such buildings may be restored in the artistic and constructional spirit of the existing fabric so that the restored building still in use should have a renewed lease of life. This is good sound practical sense and the Latin words *instaurare* or *reficere* mean exactly that: to reinstate and make anew.

*Age-value* points to an alleged aesthetic and moral requirement that the fabric of a building must "evidence the slow and inevitable disintegration of nature." The axiom of age-value, therefore, is fundamentally a modernist sensibility. Its aesthetic claim derives from the eighteenth-century picturesque tradition of the ruin while its moral overtones are inextricably linked with nineteenth-century historicism and the expectation that each and every historical period is indelibly marked by the unique spirit of its age. The collapse of a monument may be mourned but the age-value of its ruinous fabric remains superior to any restoration. Humans, this view maintains, must not tamper with time; yet it is the same ideologues of age-value who embrace the fruits of genetic medicine which, after all, aims ultimately at lengthening human life.

VIEW OF
THE VENICE
CAMPANILE

VIEW OF THE
CAPPELLA DI
SAN CATALDO
IN PALERMO

Oxford skyline

with the

Grove Buildings

of Magdalen College

in the background

*Historical value* arises when a particular monument, complex of buildings or townscape transcends over time its use and age-values by becoming a symbol that represents "the development of human activity in a certain field." Historical value, therefore, is thoroughly a social phenomenon and cannot be assigned by an individual, an expert or a ruler. Historical value depends on a shared form of life and the practices of a community within which we pick up the terms of our ethical experience. And inversely, it is our shared recognitions which empower the monument with the capacity to 'refer' to the world. Historical value, therefore, rests on recognition and its characteristic interest lies in conferring legitimacy and honour to the symbolic forms we make and which make us.

After its collapse in 1902, the Campanile of Venice was faithfully restored because in the eyes of the Venetian public the tower had immense historical value. For the London Daily Telegraph, however, the Campanile had merely an age-value and the heap of rubble it was reduced to was but a sufficient trace of the passing of time. We can see, therefore, how restoration is fraught with difficulties. The difficulties are neither technical nor financial as many would have us believe. Craftsmanship, skilled labour, precision of execution, cost of construction, imaginative talent, etc., are all mere hurdles. When a people has the requisite will all such hurdles can be surmounted.

The difficulties instead are ideological. Preservation for the sake of preserving borders on that repulsive spectacle of a blind rage for collecting the "dust of archaeological and bibliographical minutiae" described by Nietzsche. Repairing or rebuilding is in fact sensible and human but lacks the gravity of a vision. Restoration, however, presupposes real culture, not simply an art historical or archaeological knowledge of culture. Restoration cannot be pursued without such a relation to real culture.

"To restore a building," writes Viollet-le-Duc, "is not to preserve it, to repair, or rebuild it; it is to reinstate it in a condition of completeness which could never have existed at any given time."

*A version of this essay was first given as a lecture at the Art Institute of Chicago in 1995.*

Fallen

Colossal Doric

in Agrigento

# PROJECT

**TOWN OF PITIOUSA, SPETSES**

*Design Team: Demetri Porphyrios (Design Principal), Nigel Cox (Project Associate), Frank Green, Samina Shahzady (Project Architects), James Armitage, Stephen Oliver, Richard Economakis, Francis Worram, Joanna Humphries, Jason Montgomery, Duncan Moss, Charles Addison, David Cox, Taida Skaljic, David Anderson, Edwin Venn; Structural & Services Engineers: J&P Engineering; Main Contractor: J&P Construction; Photography: Leigh Simpson; Model: Jordi Fontanals; Client: 3D Development S.A.*

**DUNCAN RESIDENCE & GALLERIES, LINCOLN, NEBRASKA**

*Design Team: Demetri Porphyrios (Design Principal), Alireza Sagharchi (Project Associate), Samina Shahzady (Designer-in-charge), Darko Jazvic, Christiana Gallo, Stella Papadopoulos, Stephanie Murrill, James Armitage, Edwin Venn; Collaborating Architects and Architects of Record: Bahr, Vermeer & Haecker; Structural Engineers: R.O.Youker Inc.; Services Engineers: Olsson Associates; M&E Consultants: Fred Thompson & Associates; Main Contractor: Sampson General Contractors; Client: Mr. & Mrs. Duncan*

**VILLA AT PORTO HELI**

*Design Team: Demetri Porphyrios (Design Principal), Samina Shahzady (Designer-in-charge), Taida Skaljic, Saad Ghandour, Stella Papadopoulos, Christiana Gallo, Callum Gibb, James Armitage, Paul Rice, Edwin Venn; Collaborating Architects and Architects of Record: Andreas Zannas Architects; Structural Engineers: V. Lyrantzakis; Services Engineers: G. Lykourgiotis; Main Contractor: Emm. Koutsoudakis Ltd.*

**OLD PALACE SCHOOL, CROYDON, SURREY**

*Design Team: Demetri Porphyrios (Design Principal), Christopher Phillips (Project Associate), James Armitage (Designer-in-charge), Nigel Cox, Callum Gibb, Stephanie Murrill, Simon Lilley, Nadra Meshaka, Stella Papadopoulos, Darko Jazvic, Taida Skaljic, Richard Economakis, Edwin Venn; Project Management: The MDA Group UK; Structural Engineers: Peter Brett Associates; Quantity Surveyors: The MDA Group UK; Services Engineers: Greatorex; Client: The Whitgift Foundation*

**MAGDALEN COLLEGE, GROVE QUADRANGLE, OXFORD**

*Design Team: Demetri Porphyrios (Design Principal), Alireza Sagharchi (Project Associate), David Cox (Project Architect), Taida Skaljic, Askin Ozerin, Joanna Humphries, Edwin Venn, David Anderson; Structural Engineers: Trigram Partnership; Quantity Surveyors: Beaufort Ellis Associates; M&E Services Advisors: Styles & Whitlock; Stone Work: Ketton Architectural Stone & Masonry; Contractor: J.B. Leadbitter & Co. Ltd.; Photography: Charlotte Wood; Model: James Wink; Client: Magdalen College, Oxford*

**GONVILLE & CAIUS COLLEGE, CAMBRIDGE**

*Design Team: Demetri Porphyrios (Design Principal), Nigel Cox, (Project Associate), Richard Economakis, Stephen Oliver, David Anderson; Client: Gonville & Caius College, Cambridge*

**SELWYN COLLEGE, NEW COURTS, THEATRE & LIBRARY, CAMBRIDGE**

*Design Team: Demetri Porphyrios (Design Principal), Nigel Cox (Project Associate), Victor Deupi, James Armitage, Jason Montgomery, Simon Lilley, Darko Jazvic, Callum Gibb, Nadra Meshaka, Richard Economakis, Edwin Venn; Project Management and Quantity Surveyors: Davis, Langdon & Everest; Client: Selwyn College, Cambridge*

**RESIDENCE IN AMMAN**

*Design Team: Demetri Porphyrios (Design Principal), Nigel Cox (Project Associate), Andy Grossman (Project Architect), Samina Shahzady, Stella Papadopoulos, Donata Lawrence, Nadra Meshaka, Demetra Katsota, Simon Lilley, David Cox, James Armitage; Employer's Agent and Quantity Surveyors: Davis, Langdon & Everest; Landscape Designers: Steven Ellberg & Associates; Interior Decoration: Galerie Maison et Jardin; Design & Build Contractor: Tarmac Construction International with PRC Fewster Ltd.; Photography: Nigel Cox; Client: The Royal Court of Jordan*

**UNIVERSITY OF OXFORD, INSTITUTE FOR BUSINESS STUDIES**

*Design Team: Demetri Porphyrios (Design Principal), Alireza Sagharchi (Project Associate), Stella Papadopoulos, Taida Skaljic, Jason Montgomery, James Armitage, Richard Economakis, Edwin Venn, David Anderson; Model: Jordi Fontanals; Client: University of Oxford*

**SANE RESEARCH CENTRE, OXFORD**

*Design Team: Demetri Porphyrios (Design Principal), Nigel Cox (Project Associate), James Armitage, Johnny Holland, Edwin Venn; Structural Engineers: Trigram Partnership; Quantity Surveyors: Beaufort Ellis Associates; Services Engineers: Ralph T. King & Associates; Client: SANE*

# CREDITS

**WINDSOR RESORT, HURGHADA**

*Design Team: Demetri Porphyrios (Design Principal), Alireza Sagharchi (Project Associate), Richard Economakis (Designer-in-charge), Jason Montgomery, Taida Skaljic, Edwin Venn; Collaborating Architects and Architects of Record: Egyptian Consulting House; Client: Windsor Hotels International with Red Sea Company*

**MAGDALEN COLLEGE, SQUASH COURTS CENTRE, OXFORD**

*Design Team: Demetri Porphyrios (Design Principal), Alireza Sagharchi (Project Associate), Stephen Oliver (Project Architect), Taida Skaljic; Structural Engineers: Trigram Partnership; Quantity Surveyors: Beaufort Ellis Associates; M&E Services Advisors: Styles & Whitlock; Clerk of Works: David John; Main Contractor: Bickerton Group Plc.; Photography: Charlotte Wood; Client: Magdalen College, Oxford*

**ALLATINI MASTERPLAN, SALONICA**

*Design Team: Demetri Porphyrios (Design Principal), Alireza Sagharchi (Project Associate), Andy Grossman, Thomas Karavis (Project Architects), Richard Economakis, Nadra Meshaka, Wan Wah Chow, James Armitage, Edwin Venn; Client: 3D Development S.A.*

**KINGSTON MILLS MASTERPLAN, BRADFORD ON AVON**

*Design Team: Demetri Porphyrios (Design Principal), Alireza Sagharchi (Project Associate), Simon Lilley, Samina Shahzady, Nadra Meshaka; Consulting Engineers: Parkman; Quantity Surveyors: Norman Rourke & Partners; Client: Kingston Mills Development*

**WADI RUM FORT HOTEL, WADI RUM**

*Design Team: Demetri Porphyrios (Design Principal), Alireza Sagharchi (Project Associate), Richard Economakis (Designer-in-charge), Jason Montgomery, Edwin Venn, David Anderson; Quantity Surveyors: Davis, Langdon & Everest; Hotel Consultants: HVS International; Client: Abercrombie & Kent with Zara Investments*

**CAVO SALOMONTI MASTERPLAN, CRETE**

*Design Team: Demetri Porphyrios (Design Principal), Alireza Sagharchi (Project Associate), Victor Deupi, Edwin Venn, David Anderson; Client: 3D Development S.A.*

**THREE BRINDLEYPLACE OFFICE BUILDING, BIRMINGHAM**

*Design Team: Demetri Porphyrios (Design Principal), Alireza Sagharchi (Project Associate), Christopher Phillips (Project Architect), Darragh Lynch, Duncan Moss, Taida Skaljic, Marco Behrouzi, Johnny Holland, James Armitage, David Cox, Frank Green, Richard Economakis, Callum Gibb, David Anderson, Edwin Venn; Structural Engineers: Ove Arup & Partners; Quantity Surveyors: Davis, Langdon & Everest; Services Engineers: Ove Arup & Partners; Design & Build Contractor: HBG Kyle Stewart; Photography: Charlotte Wood; Client: Argent Development Consortium Ltd.*

**SEVEN BRINDLEYPLACE OFFICE BUILDING, BIRMINGHAM**

*Design Team: Demetri Porphyrios (Design Principal), Alireza Sagharchi (Project Associate), Callum Gibb (Designer-in-charge), Jason Montgomery, Taida Skaljic, James Armitage, Antigone Kapsali, Stella Papadopoulos, Simon Lilley; Structural Engineers: Ove Arup & Partners; Employer's Agent and Quantity Surveyors: Silk & Frazier; Services Engineers: Ove Arup & Partners; Design & Build Contractor: HBG Kyle Stewart; Client: Argent Development Consortium Ltd.*

**WINDSOR RAS NASRANI RESORT, SHARM EL-SHEIKH**

*Design Team: Demetri Porphyrios (Design Principal), Alireza Sagharchi (Project Associate), Darko Jazvic, Nadra Meshaka, Saad Ghandour, Darragh Lynch, Victor Deupi, Simon Lilley, Jason Montgomery, Marco Behrouzi, Edwin Venn; Collaborating Architects and Architects of Record: Egyptian Consulting House; Client: Windsor Hotels International with Red Sea Company*

**THE DAKIS JOANNOU COLLECTION GALLERIES, ATHENS**

*Design Team: Demetri Porphyrios (Design Principal), Samina Shahzady (Designer-in-charge), Darko Jazvic, Jason Montgomery, James Armitage, Demetra Katsota; Structural Engineers: G. Theodosiou; Structural Tent Engineers: Architen Ltd.; Services Engineers: J&P Services Engineering; Clerk of Works: George Andreou; Installation Design: Jeffrey Deitch and Dakis Joannou; Main Contractor: J&P Construction; Photography: Charlotte Wood; Client: The Dakis Joannou Collection*

FOUNDER'S GATE

IN TERMESSOS